FAST & FURIOUS

THE OFFICIAL COOKBOOK
SALUD, MI FAMILIA

Recipes by **Joshua Hake**
Written by **Tres Dean**

INSIGHT
EDITIONS

SAN RAFAEL · LOS ANGELES · LONDON

CONTENTS

INTRODUCTION ⚔

If you know anything about the Torettos, you know this: It's all about family. What started with two brothers and a sister in a small house in Los Angeles has grown into something bigger, something stronger, and something that leaves a legacy. The family spans generations, transcends international borders, and knows that when bonds run this deep, it's not just about bloodlines. It's about who you want to see waiting for you at the finish line.

Over the years, the family has bonded over fast cars, espionage, fistfights, and high-speed chases through far-flung locales. But when you take all that away, the thing that always brings them together in the best and worst of times alike is a hard-earned, well-deserved meal—enjoyed together. Toretto family cookouts have become the stuff of legend, the sort of gathering where once you've fixed your plate you've been ushered into something bigger.

It goes beyond cookouts, though. A tuna sandwich eaten over a café counter can center a driver before he makes his next move. A bag of chips can help even the toughest man keep his cool when talking to a woman he's falling for. Their fuel reflects their ever-growing, tight-knit community. And though each high-octane adventure brings these riders to the edge and far from home, a shared table helps them regroup and remain united.

What follows are fresh takes and flavorful re-creations of the dishes this family has built itself around. Whether it's a massive tray of Mi Familia BBQ Chicken (page 53) or Power-Up Homemade Granola (page 83), every recipe is best enjoyed in good company. You can labor over prep or measure spice ratios to the pinch, but what really makes a meal—especially a homemade one—taste so good is when it's shared with whomever you consider family.

SALUD,
MI FAMILIA.

TORETTO'S MARKET & CAFÉ STAPLES

Toretto's Market & Café has been an LA staple for generations. It is, in every sense, a family business. The Torettos have been serving up hearty, classic eats to the neighborhood since long before Dom and Mia were running the joint, and it's safe to say it isn't going anywhere anytime soon. Whether you're looking for a quick and tasty breakfast or some old-school LA diner staples, Toretto's Market & Café has you covered.

Sunrise Signature Sammy

They say breakfast is the most important meal of the day, and it's hard to imagine having a bad one after a savory bacon, egg, and cheese sandwich in the morning. It's been a Toretto's Market & Café favorite for years. Whether you're hitting the road or hitting the gym, it'll get your tank full for the day.

Active Time: 20 minutes

Total Time: 20 minutes

Serves: 4

8 slices thick-cut bacon

1 tablespoon butter

6 large eggs, gently whisked

Salt

Black pepper

2 cups kale leaves, torn, center rib removed

8 slices sourdough bread, toasted

4 slices white cheddar cheese

In a large skillet over medium heat, cook the bacon until crisp, turning halfway through, about 8 minutes. Remove the bacon to a paper towel–lined plate to drain.

Reduce the heat to low and add half of the butter. Pour in the eggs. Season to taste with salt and pepper. Cook, occasionally scraping the pan with a rubber spatula, until the eggs are set, 4 to 5 minutes. Remove from the heat.

In another skillet, melt the remaining butter. Add the kale and cook just until wilted, 2 to 3 minutes.

Divide the eggs among 4 slices of toast. Top with the bacon, cheese, kale, and remaining toast slices. Cut in half and serve immediately.

Pacific Coast Avocado Toast [V]

Toretto's has been slinging this quick, savory dish for years. These days, there are plenty of fancy new brunch spots in Echo Park serving up avocado toast at a higher price. But the market has had it on lock long before those trendy new spots were even on the map. You can dress this straightforward yet savory dish up or keep it simple. Either way, it's a great way to start your morning.

Active Time:
20 minutes

Total Time:
20 minutes

Serves:
4

1 tablespoon butter

4 slices multigrain bread

2 large, ripe avocados

½ lime, juiced

¼ teaspoon dried oregano

¼ teaspoon ground cumin

Salt

Black pepper

GREEK TOPPINGS

¼ cup Kalamata olives, sliced

½ cup sliced cherry tomatoes

½ cup crumbled feta or goat cheese

Basil leaves

SOUTHWEST TOPPINGS

½ cup black beans

1 cup shredded Colby-Jack cheese

¼ cup hot salsa

Cilantro leaves

In a large skillet, melt half of the butter. Add 2 slices of bread and toast until golden brown, turning once, about 5 minutes. Repeat with the remaining butter and bread.

In a medium bowl, mash the avocado with a fork into a rough paste. Fold in the lime juice, oregano, cumin, and salt and pepper to taste.

Spread mixture evenly on top of the toasts. Top with the desired toppings.

Wings, K-Town Style [GF]

The market menu features influences and flavors from all over Los Angeles. With Koreatown just a short drive from the neighborhood, adding these tangy bites to the menu was a no-brainer.

Active Time:	Total Time:	Serves:
20 minutes	1 hour 20 minutes	4

2 pounds chicken wings, flats (the middle part of the wing), and drums divided

2 tablespoons rice flour

2 teaspoons baking powder

2 teaspoons togarashi seasoning

½ cup butter

½ cup gochujang (Korean red chile paste)

½ cup water, plus more if needed

¼ cup sliced scallions

2 tablespoons toasted sesame seeds

2 tablespoons roughly chopped nori strips

Ranch dressing, for serving (optional)

Preheat the oven to 400°F. Line a large rimmed baking pan with parchment paper.

Pat the wings dry with paper towels. In a large bowl, whisk together the rice flour, baking powder, and togarashi seasoning. Toss the wings in the flour mixture to coat. Arrange on the prepared pan. Bake wings for 1 hour, turning halfway through.

While the wings are cooking, melt the butter in a medium saucepan over medium heat. Add the gochujang and whisk to combine. Add ½ cup water and whisk to combine. Heat, stirring frequently, until heated through, but do not boil. Add more water, if necessary, to achieve the desired consistency.

Transfer the wings to a large bowl and drizzle with the hot glaze. Toss to thoroughly coat. Transfer the glazed wings to a serving platter. Top with the scallions, sesame seeds, and nori. Serve with ranch dressing, if desired.

High Occupancy Veggie Quesadillas [V]

Whether you've fully cut meat out of your diet or you're just looking for a Meatless Monday option, this Toretto's Market & Café classic with an LA/Southwest flair is an easy meat-free breakfast or lunch option.

Active Time: 20 minutes

Total Time: 20 minutes

Serves: 4

1 tablespoon vegetable oil

1 red bell pepper, stemmed, seeded, and chopped

1 green bell pepper, stemmed, seeded, and chopped

½ red onion, diced

8 ounces cremini mushrooms, stemmed and sliced

1 cup diced zucchini

1 teaspoon adobo seasoning

½ teaspoon hot chile powder

½ teaspoon ground cumin

½ teaspoon black pepper

2 large flour tortillas

¾ cup shredded Monterey Jack cheese

Salsa, for serving

Sour cream, for serving

Cilantro, for garnish (optional)

In a large skillet, heat the oil over medium heat. Add the bell peppers, onion, mushrooms, and zucchini. Cook, stirring often, for 2 minutes. Add the adobo seasoning, chile powder, cumin, and black pepper. Cook, stirring frequently, until the vegetables are crisp-tender, about 3 minutes more. Transfer to a bowl or plate.

Place half of the vegetables on one half of each tortilla. Sprinkle cheese over the vegetables. Fold the tortillas in half and return to the skillet over medium-low heat. Toast until lightly browned and crisp on both sides, 3 to 4 minutes on each side.

Cut each quesadilla into 4 wedges and serve with salsa and sour cream. Sprinkle with cilantro, if desired.

Tuna Sando, No Crust

The story of Brian and Mia starts with a guy, a girl, and a tuna sandwich (a few tuna sandwiches, actually; Brian came by daily ordering one just for the chance to see Mia). Back in the day it was, in Mia's words, "crappy"—Vince wasn't kidding when he said no one liked the tuna there. Still, Brian kept ordering it anyway. Over the years, they've tweaked the recipe to get it dialed in so it's every bit the sando that sandwich lovers will come back and order every single day. Just remember: no crust.

Active Time: 20 minutes

Total Time: 20 minutes

Serves: 4

Three 5-ounce cans water-packed tuna, drained

1 tablespoon olive oil

1 small carrot, shredded

2 stalks celery, finely diced

½ red onion, finely diced

½ cup spicy pickles, finely diced

¼ cup mayonnaise

2 tablespoons stone-ground mustard

2 teaspoons apple cider vinegar

Salt

Black pepper

8 slices white bread, crusts removed

4 leaves iceberg lettuce

In a large bowl, combine the tuna, olive oil, carrot, celery, onion, pickles, mayonnaise, mustard, vinegar, and salt and pepper to taste. Use a rubber spatula to gently mix, being careful not to break up the fish too much.

Top 4 slices of bread with a leaf of iceberg lettuce. Divide the tuna mixture evenly among the lettuce leaves. Top with the remaining bread slices. Slice and serve immediately. Pair with Simple Life Potato Chips (page 33) for a great lunch.

California Republic Grilled Cheese

A warm, melty grilled cheese with crisp bacon is comfort food at its finest. Mix in seasoned chicken and it's always going to go over well. Anybody—even Uncle Vince—could manage to make it without burning the house down (though don't expect him to have washed so much as a plate after). This souped-up classic hits the spot day or night.

Active Time: 20 minutes

Total Time: 30 minutes

Serves: 4

1 tablespoon butter

8 slices white bread

8 slices double-smoked bacon

1 pound cooked chicken breast, thinly sliced

2 cups shredded Colby-Jack cheese

1 large tomato, cut into 8 slices

½ cup ranch dressing

Simple Life Potato Chips (page 33), for serving

Preheat the oven to 350°F. Line a large rimmed baking pan with parchment paper.

In a large skillet over medium heat, melt half of the butter. Add 4 slices of bread and toast lightly on both sides, about 5 minutes. Repeat with the remaining butter and bread slices. Arrange the bread slices on the prepared pan.

Add the bacon to the skillet and cook until tender-crisp, about 8 minutes. Remove the bacon to a paper towel–lined plate to drain.

Add the chicken to the skillet and toss until warmed through. Divide the chicken among 4 slices of bread. Top each with the remaining bread slices and 2 slices of bacon.

Divide the cheese among all 8 slices of toast. Bake until the cheese is melty, about 5 minutes. Remove from the oven and let cool slightly, 1 to 2 minutes.

Top the chicken-and-cheese-topped toast with 2 slices of tomato and drizzle each with 2 tablespoons of ranch dressing. Flip the bacon-and-cheese-topped toast on top and gently press the sandwich halves together.

Serve with Simple Life Potato Chips (page 33), soup, or salad.

Lemon Temptation [V]

Bring this sweet-and-tangy lemon crowd-pleaser to your next family reunion—nothing brings family together like clamoring over one another for the last slice. Torettos aren't great at resisting temptation.

Active Time: 1 hour

Total Time: 4 hours

Serves: 6 to 8

Half 14-ounce package refrigerated piecrusts	1 cup water	⅓ cup cornstarch
10 large eggs, separated, at room temperature	⅓ cup milk	½ teaspoon cream of tartar
2 cups granulated sugar, divided	⅓ cup lemon juice	Pinch salt
	2 teaspoons lemon zest	**SPECIAL EQUIPMENT**
	¼ teaspoon fine salt	Electric mixer

Preheat the oven to 450°F.

Gently place the piecrust in a 9-inch pie dish or pan. Pinch the crust to create a decorative edge. Place a round of parchment on top of the crust, with the edges of the parchment extending over the edges of the pan. Fill the bottom of pan with pie weights or dried beans. Bake for 10 minutes. Remove the parchment with weights and bake until golden, 5 to 6 minutes more. Turn the oven to 350°F.

While the crust bakes, make the filling. In a large bowl, whisk the egg yolks; set aside. In a medium saucepan, combine 1½ cups of sugar, the water, milk, lemon juice and zest, salt, and cornstarch. Cook, whisking frequently, over medium heat until thickened, 5 to 7 minutes. Remove from the heat, and reduce oven to 350°F.

Whisk 3 tablespoons of the sugar-milk mixture into the egg yolks. Slowly pour the egg mixture into the remaining sugar-milk mixture, whisking constantly. Return the pan to medium-low heat and cook, whisking constantly, until large bubbles form, 2 to 3 minutes. Cover and remove from the heat.

For the meringue, in a large bowl, beat the egg whites and cream of tartar with an electric mixer on medium to combine. Turn the mixer to high and beat until soft peaks form, 4 to 5 minutes. Add the remaining ½ cup of sugar and a pinch of salt and beat until stiff peaks form, 2 to 3 minutes more.

Pour the warm lemon mixture into the pre-baked crust. Use a rubber spatula to spread meringue over the lemon mixture all the way to the crust, creating decorative ridges and curls with the meringue. Bake until the meringue is lightly golden brown in spots.

Let cool on a wire rack for 1 hour, then transfer to the refrigerator for 3 hours to chill before serving.

East Coast Cannoli [V]

The Toretto family is Los Angeles born and raised, but this hard-to-resist staple of New York delis made its way into the café and never left. Once you're family, you're family.

Active Time: 35 minutes

Total Time: 1 hour

Serves: 6

1 cup all-purpose flour, plus more for dusting

1 tablespoon cold butter, cubed

1 teaspoon granulated sugar

Pinch salt

1 large egg, beaten

¼ cup red wine

One 15-ounce container ricotta cheese

½ cup powdered sugar, plus more for garnish

1 cup frozen whipped topping, thawed

½ teaspoon vanilla extract

½ teaspoon maple syrup

Vegetable oil, for frying

Cinnamon, for garnish

Chocolate syrup, for garnish

In a medium bowl, use your hands to mix the flour, butter, granulated sugar, and salt, squeezing the butter with the flour to combine. Add half of the beaten egg and the wine and mix to form a dough ball. Cover and let rest in the refrigerator 30 minutes.

While the dough rests, place the ricotta in a fine-mesh strainer. Gently press with the back of a spoon over the sink to get rid of excess water. Transfer to a medium bowl. Add the powdered sugar, whipped topping, vanilla, and maple syrup. Stir to combine, then spoon into a pastry bag.

Store in the refrigerator until ready to use.

In a Dutch oven, heat 3 inches of oil to 375°F over medium heat. Lightly dust a clean work surface with flour. Roll out the dough ball into a thin sheet about ⅛ inch thick. Use a 3- to 3½-inch biscuit cutter to make 12 rounds. Carefully roll, not too tightly, around the cannoli mold, using your finger to brush a small amount of the remaining beaten egg along the top inside edge of the dough to seal. Pull ends of dough out slightly.

Fry in batches until brown and bubbly, rolling gently to cook evenly, 2 to 3 minutes. Remove from the pan. Holding the cannoli mold with tongs, gently twist off the cannoli using a hot pad. Place on a wire rack to cool completely.

When ready to serve, pipe filling into the cannoli shells, starting in the middle and filling from each side. Sprinkle with cinnamon and powdered sugar. Drizzle with chocolate syrup and serve immediately.

HIT THE ROAD

Maybe you're hitting the road for a cross-country trip or maybe you're just driving down the street to get some gym time in before work. Wherever your drive takes you, you'll need to fuel up as much as your ride. Nobody likes to drive hungry. These recipes are all handheld, portable provisions. We can't promise they won't make a mess, though—no matter where the road takes us, potholes happen.

Full-Tank Fruit Plate [V, V+, GF]

When you're in a rush and need a quick, light boost before setting out on the road, this high-octane fruit plate has you covered. There's no time to feel weighed down when one of the crew needs a heroic rescue.

Active Time: 20 minutes

Total Time: 1 hour 20 minutes

Serves: 6

2 ripe mangoes, pitted, peeled, and cubed

2 cups cubed fresh pineapple

2 cups cubed watermelon

1 cup strawberries, stemmed and halved

1 English cucumber, cut into ½-inch-thick half-moons

1 cup fresh blackberries

1 tablespoon Tajín® seasoning

1 tablespoon dark brown sugar

Juice and zest of 1 lime

2 tablespoons chopped fresh basil

In a large bowl, combine the mangoes, pineapple, watermelon, strawberries, cucumber, and blackberries. Add the Tajín seasoning, brown sugar, and lime juice and zest. Cover and chill in the refrigerator for 1 hour.

To serve, toss and transfer to a serving platter. Sprinkle with fresh basil.

Fast Break Breakfast Burritos

The debate over which state ranks best for burritos is never going to end, but if you ask the Toretto family, this tantalizing recipe is the end-all-be-all argument in favor of California burritos.

Active Time: 30 minutes

Total Time: 30 minutes

Serves: 4

1 pound breakfast sausage

2 cups frozen hash browns

1 teaspoon butter

1 red onion, chopped

1 green bell pepper, stemmed, seeded, and chopped

6 large eggs, beaten

Salt

Black pepper

⅔ cup black beans, warmed

1 cup shredded cheddar cheese

4 burrito-size flour tortillas

Salsa, for serving

Heat a large nonstick skillet over medium heat. Add the sausage and cook until browned and crisp, breaking into crumbles with a spatula as it cooks, 8 to 10 minutes. Transfer the sausage to a paper towel–lined plate to drain.

Add the hash browns to the skillet. Let cook for 5 minutes without stirring. Flip and cook for 5 more minutes or until browned on both sides and cooked through. Transfer to a plate.

Add the butter, onion, and bell pepper to the skillet. Cook the vegetables until crisp-tender, 3 to 4 minutes. Remove from the skillet. Add the beaten eggs and season with salt and pepper to taste. Cook, stirring frequently, until the eggs are fluffy. Remove skillet from the heat.

Divide the sausage, hash browns, eggs, vegetables, beans, and cheese among the tortillas. Fold in the sides of the tortillas over the fillings, then fold in the edge closest to you. Roll up.

Place the skillet over medium heat. Place the tortillas, fold-side down, in the skillet. Toast until sealed, 3 to 4 minutes. Use tongs to turn, then toast on the other side 3 to 4 minutes. Serve with salsa.

TIP

To eat on the road, wrap untoasted burritos in foil and freeze in a large zip-top freezer bag. When ready to eat, remove from the foil and heat in the microwave for 2 to 3 minutes or until hot. Rewrap in foil and take along lots of napkins.

Simple Life Potato Chips [V, GF]

Han started crushing potato chips after he quit smoking and craved a crunchy, salty distraction, which Gisele noticed right away. Many of the family's love stories began over food. Like the ever-growing Toretto family, this recipe has evolved also, including LA-style flavors that everyone is sure to crave.

Active Time: 30 minutes

Total Time: 1 hour

Serves: 10

8 Yukon Gold potatoes

1½ quarts vegetable oil

3 tablespoons smoked salt

1 cup sour cream

2 tablespoons vinegar-based hot sauce

Slice the potatoes very thinly and place in a large bowl of ice water as you work to prevent browning. Let stand 30 minutes, then drain and place on large, paper towel–lined baking pans (as many as needed to allow the potatoes to drain in a single layer). Pat very dry with more paper towels.

In a Dutch oven, heat the oil to 275°F over medium-high heat.

Cook the potatoes in the hot oil in batches, turning occasionally, until golden brown, about 10 minutes, allowing the oil to come back up to 275°F after each batch. Remove with a metal mesh or kitchen spider to paper towel–lined pans (use fresh towels). Sprinkle immediately with smoked salt.

To serve, stir together the sour cream and hot sauce in a small bowl. Serve with the chips for dipping.

TIP For the thinnest, mostly evenly sliced potatoes, use a mandoline slicer to cut ⅟₁₆ inch thick. The cooking time will be shorter, so watch carefully.

Grab 'n' Go Empanadas

A longtime cornerstone of LA street food and a favorite of the original Toretto crew, an empanada is the perfect grab 'n' go fare. Whether as a quick snack or a lunch you can eat on the go, its savory flavors will satisfy your cravings, especially when you're in a race to get somewhere.

Active Time: 1 hour

Total Time: 1 hour 40 minutes

Serves: 6

FOR THE DOUGH
3 cups all-purpose flour, plus more for dusting

½ teaspoon salt

½ cup cold butter, cubed

1 egg, room temperature

¾ cup ice water

FOR THE FILLING
1 tablespoon butter

1 pound ground pork

1 white onion, finely diced

1 cup cremini mushrooms, stemmed and finely diced

1 tablespoon ancho chile flakes

1 teaspoon chile de árbol flakes

2 teaspoons minced fresh oregano

1 teaspoon ground cumin

1 large clove garlic, minced

¼ cup chopped green olives

Salt

Black pepper

2 large eggs

1 teaspoon water

SPECIAL EQUIPMENT
Food processor

FOR THE DOUGH: In a food processor, pulse the flour and salt to combine. Add the butter and egg. Pulse just until the butter is in large chunks. Add the water, a tablespoon or two at a time, pulsing after each addition, to a mixture the size of small peas. Turn the dough out onto a work surface and gather up into a ball. Wrap in plastic and chill in the refrigerator for 30 minutes.

FOR THE FILLING: In a large skillet over medium heat, melt the butter. Add the pork and break into small crumbles. Add the onion and mushrooms. Cook, stirring occasionally, for 10 minutes; drain the fat. Add the ancho chile, chile de árbol, oregano, cumin, garlic, olives, and salt and pepper to taste. Cook for an additional 5 minutes. Remove from the heat and cool.

Preheat the oven to 375°F. Line a large rimmed baking pan with parchment.

Lightly dust a work surface with flour. Divide dough into 18 balls and roll flat with rolling pin. Divide filling among centers of flattened dough balls.

Whisk the eggs with water and lightly brush around the outsides of the dough circles. Fold the dough in half over the filling and seal with the tines of a fork. Place on the prepared baking pan. Lightly brush with the remaining egg wash over the tops.

Bake until golden brown, about 30 minutes.

"Wrap It Up" Chicken Caesar Salad

When you've really gotta burn rubber, this tasty, healthy wrap is the move. It'll leave you satisfied for every inch of that quarter-mile race.

Active Time:
15 minutes

Total Time:
15 minutes

Serves:
4

4 large spinach or tomato flour tortillas

4 cups shredded romaine lettuce

½ cup bottled Caesar dressing

Coarse-ground black pepper

1½ pounds sliced grilled chicken breast

1 cup croutons, lightly crushed

½ cup shredded Parmesan cheese

Lay the tortillas on a work surface. In a large bowl, toss the lettuce with the Caesar dressing. Season to taste with the black pepper. Divide the dressed lettuce among the tortillas. Top with the chicken, croutons, and Parmesan cheese.

Roll the tortilla up burrito style so it's easy to handle, and serve.

Gallo's Pizzeria Slice [V]

Agent Dunn brought Gallo's to the crew's attention when he was working with Brian down in South Beach. Though Miami may not exactly be a pizza hot spot, they sling a mean slice—thin crust, generous cut, and the perfect sauce-to-cheese ratio. Now you can re-create this mouthwatering masterpiece for your crew.

Active Time:
30 minutes

Total Time:
45 minutes
+ 24 hours rising time

Serves:
6

4 cups bread flour, plus more for dusting

1 tablespoon granulated sugar

1 tablespoon salt

1½ teaspoons active dry yeast

2½ tablespoons olive oil

1½ cups warm water

2 cups marinara sauce

8 cups shredded low-moisture part-skim mozzarella cheese

2 teaspoons Italian seasoning

SPECIAL EQUIPMENT
Food processor

Two 16-inch round pizza pans

In a food processor, combine the flour, sugar, salt, and yeast. Pulse a few times to combine. Add the olive oil and water and pulse until a ball forms. Process for 10 to 15 more seconds.

Knead the dough on a work surface lightly dusted with flour until smooth, about 2 minutes. Divide into 2 equal portions and place each in a gallon-size zip-top bag. Chill in the refrigerator for 24 hours.

Preheat the oven to 450°F.

Line two 16-inch-round pizza pans with parchment paper. Roll out the dough balls into 14-inch circles and place on the prepared pans. Evenly divide the marinara sauce between the dough circles. Sprinkle with the cheese and Italian seasoning.

Bake until the cheese is bubbly and the crust is dark golden brown, about 15 minutes.

Sweet Tooth Churros [V]

The next time you're on the road and crave a sweet treat, ditch the gas station doughnut. Pack these bite-size homemade confections instead to satisfy anyone with a sweet tooth and high-energy streak like Roman. Maybe he'd grind the gang's gears a little less if he kept a bag of these little delicacies in his center console.

Active Time:
30 minutes

Total Time:
35 minutes

Serves:
4

1 quart vegetable oil

1 cup water

¼ cup butter

¼ cup plus 1 tablespoon sugar, divided

¼ teaspoon salt

1 cup all-purpose flour

½ teaspoon vanilla extract

¼ teaspoon ground nutmeg

1¼ teaspoons ground cinnamon, divided

1 large egg

¼ teaspoon cayenne pepper

SPECIAL EQUIPMENT
Piping bag with star tip

In a Dutch oven, preheat the oil to 350°F over medium-high heat.

In a large saucepan, bring the water, butter, 1 tablespoon sugar, and the salt to a boil. Add the flour. Reduce the heat to low and stir with a rubber spatula, scraping the sides of the pan to combine.

Add the vanilla, nutmeg, ¼ teaspoon cinnamon, and the egg. Blend with an electric mixer until smooth. Let cool for 5 minutes. Transfer to a large piping bag fitted with a star tip.

Pipe 8-inch segments of dough into the oil. Cut each 8-inch segment in half with kitchen scissors and fry for 4 minutes, turning halfway through. Drain on a large, paper towel–lined baking pan. Repeat with the remaining dough, allowing oil to come back up to 350°F between batches.

In a small bowl, combine the remaining ¼ cup sugar, remaining 1 teaspoon cinnamon, and the cayenne. Sprinkle over the warm churros.

FOR THE COOKOUT

If there's one thing the family knows, it's that there's nothing like breaking bread over a mean spread with your loved ones. They've hosted cookouts to celebrate victories, make amends, and welcome new family into the fold. With classic recipes abound, new additions to the family tend to start new traditions. What follows are some family-gathering must-haves. Serve them up for friends and family alike, and always be grateful for the occasion—and the company.

Shrimp for the Table [GF]

Sometimes you've gotta throw together a cookout on short notice after trotting around the globe and saving the world a time—or ten—and you don't have a lot of time to plan a menu. When those times come, this recipe is your friend. It's easy to prep and universally enjoyed. Peel-and-eat shrimp get a barbecue started on the best possible note.

Active Time:	Total Time:	Serves:
30 minutes	1 hour 30 minutes	6

FOR THE SHRIMP
2 pounds easy-peel (shell on, deveined) jumbo shrimp

1 tablespoon salt

1 tablespoon sugar

½ teaspoon baking soda

4 cups water

Two 12-ounce cans pilsner beer

3 stalks celery, coarsely chopped

1 yellow onion, coarsely chopped

2 carrots, sliced

2 cloves garlic, smashed

4 sprigs fresh thyme

1 lemon, halved

FOR THE SAUCES
2 cups cocktail sauce

3 tablespoons prepared horseradish

1 cup sweet chile sauce

1 cup orange preserves or marmalade

1 tablespoon red pepper flakes

FOR SERVING
Lemon wedges

FOR THE SHRIMP: Rinse the shrimp and pat dry. In a large bowl, toss the shrimp with the salt, sugar, and baking soda. Chill in the refrigerator for 1 hour.

In a large pot, combine the water, beer, celery, onion, carrots, garlic, thyme, and lemon halves. Bring to a boil over medium-high heat, then let simmer until the shrimp are done resting in the refrigerator.

Pour the shrimp into a large bowl through a strainer. Return the liquid to the pot; discard the solids.

Heat the reserved liquid to just below a simmer, around 180°F. Remove the shrimp from the refrigerator and add it directly to the poaching liquid. Stirring constantly, cook the shrimp until no longer translucent, 3 to 5 minutes. Remove the shrimp from the poaching liquid with a slotted spoon and lay on a large rimmed baking pan. Place in the freezer to cool for 5 minutes, then transfer to the refrigerator.

FOR THE SAUCES: In a small serving bowl, stir together the cocktail sauce and horseradish. In a second serving bowl, stir together the sweet chile sauce, orange preserves, and red pepper flakes.

FOR SERVING: Serve the shrimp with the sauces and lemon wedges.

Iceberg Salad [GF]

Like the opening scene of a film, the first course sets the tone for your dining event, and this classic iceberg salad is a fresh opener for every backyard barbecue. Full of healthy greens, good-for-you ingredients, and classic tastebud tantalizers, guests can customize this crisp, cool salad however they want.

Active Time: 15 minutes

Total Time: 20 minutes

Serves: 4

1 large head iceberg lettuce, quartered

2 tablespoons vegetable oil

½ cup bottled ranch dressing

1 avocado, pitted and thinly sliced

1 cup cherry tomatoes, quartered

⅓ cup banana pepper rings

¾ cup blue cheese crumbles

½ cup dry-roasted pepitas

½ cup cooked crumbled bacon

1 teaspoon paprika

Preheat the grill to medium-high.

Rub the cut sides of the lettuce wedges with oil. Grill the lettuce until lightly charred, about 2 minutes on each side. Place 1 wedge on each of 4 serving plates. Gently fan out the lettuce leaves.

Drizzle each wedge with the ranch dressing. Top with the avocado slices, tomatoes, banana pepper rings, blue cheese crumbles, pepitas, and bacon—or any mix of toppings as desired. Sprinkle with paprika and serve.

Mi Familia BBQ Chicken

It doesn't matter which coast you're on, barbecue chicken is the centerpiece of every traditional American cookout. The Toretto family's spread is constantly evolving, but this classic is always on the table. It was served when Brian first joined the crew and even when the team celebrated Han's mysteriously miraculous return. Whether you're celebrating milestones or the blessing of having your family together in the same place, a timeless favorite certainly commemorates the occasion.

Active Time: | **Total Time:** | **Serves:**
1 hour 5 minutes | 1 hour 25 minutes | 6

2 quarts water

2 tablespoons salt

2 tablespoons sugar

Juice of 2 lemons

8 sprigs fresh thyme

6 chicken hindquarters

2 tablespoons vegetable oil

2 teaspoons salt

1 teaspoon black pepper

1 cup ketchup

2 tablespoons sambal oelek

2 tablespoons brown sugar

1 tablespoon Worcestershire sauce

1 teaspoon chile powder

In a large pot, whisk the water, salt, and sugar until dissolved, 3 to 4 minutes. Add the lemon juice and thyme, then add the chicken. Chill in the refrigerator for 1 hour.

Preheat the grill to medium. Remove the chicken from the brine and pat dry. Rub with oil and season with salt and pepper to taste.

In a medium bowl, combine the ketchup, sambal oelek, brown sugar, Worcestershire sauce, and chile powder. Set aside.

Place the chicken on the grill. Turn after 1 minute, then again after another 1 minute. Turn two more times every 5 minutes, for a total of 20 minutes. Lightly brush with the sauce. Grill for 10 minutes, then brush again with the sauce. Grill until the internal temperature reaches 165°F, about 30 more minutes, turning once.

Brush with the remaining sauce.

Slow & Sweet BBQ Ribs [GF]

When this customary course hits the grill and the sweet, smoky aroma starts drifting through the air, you know the meal is getting kicked up a notch. Just have plenty of napkins on hand—you don't want anybody smearing sauce all over your car's souped-up interior.

Active Time: 30 minutes   **Total Time:** 2 hours 30 minutes   **Serves:** 4

¼ cup brown sugar

2 teaspoons seasoned salt

1 teaspoon smoked paprika

1 teaspoon black pepper

½ teaspoon ground cinnamon

½ teaspoon red pepper flakes

1 rack baby back ribs, membrane removed

½ cup favorite bottled barbecue sauce

¼ cup apple cider vinegar

¼ cup blueberry jam

Preheat the grill to medium-low.

In a small bowl, combine the brown sugar, seasoned salt, paprika, black pepper, cinnamon, and red pepper flakes. Rub all over the ribs. Loosely wrap the ribs in two layers of aluminum foil, and place on the grill. Cook for 2 hours, turning every 30 minutes.

While the ribs cook, in a small saucepan, combine the barbecue sauce, vinegar, and blueberry jam. Cook over medium heat, stirring frequently, until reduced by half, about 10 minutes.

Unwrap the ribs and return to the grill, bone-side down. Brush with the barbecue sauce a few times, allowing the sauce to cook down between applications, until completely coated. Cook for 10 minutes more. Cut between the bones and serve.

Roadside Stand Italian Sausage

Just about anywhere in the world the team has found themselves, there's probably been a streetside grill sizzling close by, drawing in anyone with a hankering for local flavor. Inspired by roadside carts from around the globe, these street-style sausage and buns can throw any gathering into overdrive.

Active Time: 20 minutes

Total Time: 20 minutes

Serves: 4

4 links sweet or hot Italian sausage

Olive oil cooking spray, for greasing the sausages

1 tablespoon butter

1 red bell pepper, stemmed, seeded, and sliced

1 green bell pepper, stemmed, seeded, and sliced

½ white onion, sliced

4 hoagie rolls, split lengthwise on the hoagie tops

¾ cup giardiniera

8 slices provolone cheese

1 tablespoon Italian seasoning, for serving

Preheat the grill to medium-high heat on one side and medium on the other. Place a cast-iron skillet over medium heat.

Lightly spray the sausages with cooking spray and place on the grill. Cook for 3 minutes. Turn and cook the sausages until the internal temperature reaches 165°F, about 5 minutes more.

After the first turn of the sausages, add the butter, bell peppers, and onion to the skillet. Cook, stirring occasionally, until crisp-tender, about 5 minutes.

Turn the broiler to low. Place the sausages in hoagie rolls on a large rimmed baking pan. Top with the pepper mixture, giardiniera, and cheese. Broil until the cheese is bubbly and the bread is lightly toasted, about 4 minutes.

Sprinkle with Italian seasoning and serve.

LA Drive-Through Double Burgers

If it isn't broken, don't fix it. And burgers cooked on a grill outdoors? That ain't broken. Los Angeles is the drive-through capital of America, and the charbroiled smoky scent lingering in the air on the block of every burger joint is almost as mouthwatering as the aromas of a Toretto cookout drifting across their East LA neighborhood.

Active Time: 25 minutes

Total Time: 25 minutes

Serves: 4

FOR THE SAUCE
2 tablespoons ketchup

2 tablespoons mayonnaise

2 tablespoons sweet pickle relish

FOR THE BURGERS
4 sesame seed buns

Softened butter, for greasing the buns

1 tablespoon vegetable oil

1 pound ground beef, divided into eight 2-ounce balls

Salt

Black pepper

8 slices American cheese

1 cup shredded iceberg lettuce

1 tomato, sliced

½ white onion, thinly sliced

FOR THE SAUCE: In a small bowl, stir together ketchup, mayonnaise, and relish; set aside.

FOR THE BURGERS: Brush the cut sides of the buns with softened butter. Heat a cast-iron griddle or flattop grill over high heat. Toast the buttered sides of the buns until lightly golden brown, about 1 minute. Set aside.

Spread oil on the griddle. Place the beef balls 4 inches apart on the griddle. (You may need to work in batches if you have a small griddle.) Press down firmly on the beef balls to flatten them wider than the buns. Season with salt and pepper to taste. Cook the patties until browned and the edges are beginning to char, about 4 minutes.

Using a metal spatula, flip the patties. Top each patty with a cheese slice. Cook until the cheese begins to melt, about 1 minute more. Spread burger sauce on the buns' tops and bottoms. Divide the lettuce among the bun bottoms. Stack the burgers 2 patties tall, and place them on the bottom buns. Top with the tomato, onion, and bun tops.

Street-Style LA Tacos

The family's origins are in the City of Angels, where the street taco reigns supreme. It's a city where taco spots vastly outnumber burger joints, and there are just as many ways to serve them up. But if you want to really bring a little LA flavor to your spread, try making tacos with these authentic flavors and fillings.

Active Time: 30 minutes

Total Time: 2 hours 30 minutes

Serves: 6

3 tablespoons tamari or soy sauce

Juice and zest of 1 lime

2 cloves garlic, minced

1 tablespoon chopped fresh oregano

1 teaspoon ground cumin

2 pounds skirt steak or flap steak

Olive oil cooking spray, for greasing the grill

18 mini corn tortillas

1 white onion, finely diced

1 cup cilantro leaves

2 limes, cut into wedges

Hot sauce, for serving

Cotija cheese, for serving

In a medium bowl, whisk together the tamari, lime juice and zest, garlic, oregano, and cumin. Place the steak in a gallon-size zip-top bag, and pour the marinade over the meat. Seal the bag and place it in a bowl. Refrigerate for 2 hours.

Preheat the grill to medium-high. Spray the grates with cooking spray. Grill the steak to medium doneness, 8 to 10 minutes, turning every 2 minutes. Remove from the grill and let rest 5 minutes. Cut into bite-size pieces.

Heat an extra-large skillet over medium heat. Pour in the reserved marinade and simmer for 3 minutes to reduce slightly. Add the chopped steak and cook about 2 minutes more.

Place 3 tortillas each on 6 serving plates. Divide the meat evenly among the tortillas. Top with the onion and cilantro. Serve with lime wedges, hot sauce, and cotija cheese.

Hot Rods & Street Dogs

Car meets are hot spots for vendors serving bacon-wrapped hot dogs or spicy sausages perfectly complemented by piping-hot grilled peppers and onions. It's a West Coast essential, from Dodgers games to Forum concerts. But you don't have to travel all the way to LA for a taste once you toss a few of these on the table.

Active Time: **Total Time:**   **Serves:**

    30 minutes   2 hours 30 minutes   6

4 beef hot dogs	2 jalapeño peppers, sliced
4 slices bacon	1 tomato, diced
1 teaspoon vegetable oil	2 tablespoons hot mustard
1 sweet onion, half diced, half cut into slivers	2 tablespoons mayonnaise
1 cup canned refried beans, warmed	Hot sauce, for serving
4 hot dog buns	

Preheat the oven to 400°F. Line a large rimmed baking pan with foil.

Wrap the hot dogs in bacon, securing the ends with toothpicks. Place on the prepared pan and bake for 8 minutes, turning halfway through the cooking time.

Heat a large skillet over medium heat. Add the oil and diced onion. Cook until lightly browned, about 5 minutes. Remove from the skillet.

Transfer the bacon-wrapped hot dogs to the skillet. Cook, turning occasionally, until the bacon is crisp, about 5 minutes. Remove the toothpicks.

Spread the refried beans on the bun bottoms. Place the hot dogs on the beans. Top with sliced jalapeños, diced tomato, slivered onions, mustard, and mayonnaise.

Serve with hot sauce.

K-Town Tacos

Los Angeles is a melting pot of cultures and cuisines, and sometimes that results in culinary alchemy. Such is the case with the Korean taco—it's a delicious fusion of cultures, like Dom's ever-growing family.

Active Time: 30 minutes

Total Time: 40 minutes

Serves: 4

FOR THE CHICKEN
8 boneless, skinless chicken thighs

¼ cup gochujang (Korean red chile paste)

¼ cup soy sauce

2 tablespoons brown sugar

1 tablespoon garlic paste

1 teaspoon toasted sesame oil

FOR THE SLAW
2 cups shredded red cabbage

1 red pear, diced

1 mango, pitted, peeled, and diced

2 teaspoons gochugaru (Korean chile flakes)

1 teaspoon honey

FOR SERVING
Eight 6-inch flour tortillas

4 scallions, sliced on the bias

2 tablespoons toasted sesame seeds

FOR THE CHICKEN: Heat the oven to broil. Line a large rimmed baking pan with foil. Place an oven-safe metal rack on the pan.

Trim the chicken thighs of any excess fat. In a small bowl, whisk together the gochujang, soy sauce, brown sugar, garlic paste, and sesame oil. Place the chicken in a gallon-size zip-top bag. Pour the marinade over the chicken; seal and massage to coat. Let marinate at room temperature for 20 minutes.

FOR THE SLAW: While the chicken marinates, in a large bowl, combine the cabbage, pear, mango, gochugaru, and honey. Toss to combine and set aside.

Arrange the chicken thighs on the metal rack, and broil for 5 minutes. Turn and broil for 5 minutes more. Let rest for 5 to 10 minutes, then thinly slice.

FOR SERVING: Divide the chicken among the tortillas. Top with the slaw and garnish with scallions and sesame seeds.

Pedal to the Metal Mariscos [GF]

This delicious, savory seafood stew brimming with shrimp, halibut, crab legs, and clams captures the spirit of the Baja Coast spicing up any outdoor gathering.

Active Time: 45 minutes

Total Time: 1 hour 5 minutes

Serves: 4 to 6

1 tablespoon vegetable oil

1 white onion, chopped

2 stalks celery, sliced

1 jalapeño, chopped

1 tomato, quartered

One 6-inch corn tortilla, plus more for serving

4 cups water

1 tablespoon vegetable bouillon paste

2 tablespoons butter

1 teaspoon paprika

½ cup dry white wine

1 cup spicy tomato juice

1 pound shrimp, peeled and deveined

1 pound snow crab legs

1 pound littleneck clams

1 pound halibut, cut into 1-inch chunks

Salt

Black pepper

Cilantro, for serving

Lime wedges, for serving

Pico de gallo, for serving

In a large pot, heat the vegetable oil over medium-high heat. Add the onion, celery, jalapeño, and tomato. Cook, stirring until the vegetables are slightly roasted, about 5 minutes. Transfer to a blender. Toast the tortilla in a pan, turning once, being careful not to burn it. Place in a blender with the vegetables.

Add the water and bouillon paste to the blender. Blend until smooth and return to the pot. Add the butter, paprika, wine, and tomato juice. Bring to a simmer. Add the shrimp, crab legs, clams, and halibut. Simmer, stirring occasionally, until the seafood is cooked through, being careful not to break up the fish too much, about 15 minutes. Season to taste with salt and pepper. Serve with the cilantro, lime wedges, pico de gallo, and corn tortillas.

Toretto Family Cornbread [V]

Like families, cornbread comes in so many varieties—some are sweet, some are flaky, some are cornier than others. No matter the style, every recipe reflects the family that makes it. This cornbread sets itself apart with a kiss of brown sugar.

Active Time:
10 minutes

Total Time:
50 minutes

Serves:
8

⅓ cup vegetable oil, plus more for greasing the pan

1 cup stone-ground cornmeal

1 cup all-purpose flour

½ cup granulated sugar

¼ cup light brown sugar

3 teaspoons baking powder

¾ teaspoon salt

1 large egg, beaten

1¼ cups buttermilk

¾ cup frozen corn, thawed and drained

Preheat the oven to 400°F. Lightly grease a 9-by-9-inch baking dish with vegetable oil.

In a medium bowl, whisk together the cornmeal, flour, sugar, brown sugar, baking powder, and salt. In a small bowl, whisk together the egg, buttermilk, and the cup of oil. Make a well in the dry ingredients. Add the wet ingredients and stir with a rubber spatula just until combined. Fold in the corn. Let stand for 10 minutes.

Pour the batter into the prepared pan. Bake for 20 minutes or until golden brown. Cool on a wire rack for 10 minutes before cutting.

Inseparable Mac 'n' Cheese [V]

This rich, creamy mac 'n' cheese pulls the family together like gravity. Like how Dom is drawn to Letty, or Brian to Mia—when two things are meant to go together, they make a great combination. The same is true of this recipe. There's something about mixing warm pasta with melty, gooey cheese and Italian breadcrumbs that just makes sense.

Active Time: 30 minutes

Total Time: 50 minutes

Serves: 6

12 ounces elbow macaroni

⅓ cup butter

¼ cup all-purpose flour

2 cups milk

One 8-ounce package cream cheese, cubed

One 8-ounce block cheddar cheese, shredded

1 teaspoon salt

¼ teaspoon black pepper

½ teaspoon garlic powder

Nonstick cooking spray, for greasing the casserole dish

¼ cup grated Parmesan cheese

¼ cup Italian-seasoned breadcrumbs

3 tablespoons roughly chopped parsley

Preheat the oven to 375°F.

Cook the macaroni according to the package instructions, less 1 minute cooking time. Drain well and set aside.

In a large pot, melt the butter. Whisk in the flour. Continue to cook and whisk constantly until the mixture thickens, about 1 minute. Add the milk and cream cheese and cook, whisking frequently, until the cream cheese melts and is fully incorporated. Add the cheddar cheese, a handful at a time, whisking after each addition. Whisk in the salt, pepper, and garlic powder. Stir in the drained pasta.

Spray a 7-by-11-inch casserole dish with nonstick spray. Transfer the macaroni and cheese mixture to the dish. In a small bowl, combine the Parmesan cheese and breadcrumbs. Top the macaroni and cheese with the breadcrumb mixture.

Bake the mac and cheese until bubbly and the breadcrumb mixture is golden brown, about 20 minutes.

Let stand for 5 minutes. Sprinkle with parsley and serve.

10-Second Slaw [V, GF]

Like Dom going from 0 to 60, dress up your cookout spread fast with this recipe. Whether you're serving it as a side dish or a condiment, slaw is a refreshing essential you can easily add to any meal. It brings a touch of tartness and crunch and is great on its own or to top off the Down South BBQ Sandwich (page 38).

Active Time: 15 minutes   **Total Time:** 20 minutes   **Serves:** 6

3 cups shredded green cabbage

2 cups shredded red cabbage

1 tablespoon coarse salt

1 tablespoon Dijon mustard

1 bunch scallions, sliced

2 carrots, shredded

½ cup mayonnaise

2 tablespoons apple cider vinegar

1 teaspoon granulated sugar

1 teaspoon celery seed

½ teaspoon black pepper

In a large bowl, toss the green and red cabbage with the salt. Squeeze firmly with your hands to crunch the cabbage and distribute the salt. Transfer to a strainer over the sink and let stand for 15 minutes.

Transfer the cabbage mixture to a large bowl. Add the mustard, scallions, carrots, mayonnaise, vinegar, sugar, celery seed, and black pepper. Stir well to combine.

Serve immediately, or cover and chill in the refrigerator for 2 hours.

Overdrive Elotes [V, GF]

You haven't had corn on the cob until you've dressed it up and grilled it like this crew does—LA style, influenced by Mexican street food traditions. Elotes are a unique addition to traditional American cookout fare.

Active Time: 25 minutes

Total Time: 25 minutes

Serves: 4

⅔ cup Mexican crema

2 cloves garlic, crushed

Juice and zest of 1 lime

½ teaspoon smoked paprika

½ teaspoon chipotle powder

½ teaspoon black pepper

4 sweet corns on the cob, silk removed, husks pulled back but not removed

½ cup cilantro leaves

½ cup cotija cheese

Lime wedges, for serving (optional)

Tajín seasoning, for serving (optional)

Preheat the grill to high. In a small bowl, whisk together the crema, garlic, lime juice and zest, paprika, chipotle powder, and black pepper; set aside.

Place the corn on the grill, leaving the stalk and husks off the heat to avoid burning (the stalk will be used as a "handle" for eating the corn). Grill the corn until it begins to char, turning occasionally, 10 to 12 minutes. Remove from the grill.

Spread the crema mixture evenly onto the corn. Sprinkle with the cotija and cilantro. Serve with lime wedges and Tajín seasoning, if desired.

Plenty to Share Potato Salad [V, GF]

Potato salad is the sort of side dish you can bring to dinner for four or forty (perfect for the Toretto family, because there's no telling who or how many will show up). This recipe will send all of your guests home with full, satisfied stomachs.

Active Time: 15 minutes **Total Time:** 20 minutes **Serves:** 6

3 large eggs

2 pounds multicolored fingerling potatoes

½ cup mayonnaise

1 tablespoon stone-ground mustard

2 stalks celery, diced

½ small red onion, diced small

2 tablespoons dill pickle relish

1 teaspoon chopped fresh dill

1 teaspoon white vinegar

½ teaspoon garlic salt

¼ teaspoon celery seed

Salt

Black pepper

Heat a large and a small pot of water over high heat. When the small pot is boiling, add the eggs. Remove from the heat. Cover and let stand for 12 minutes. When the large pot is boiling, add the potatoes. Cook until fork-tender, about 10 minutes.

When the eggs are done, place in cool water. Peel and chop the eggs and place in a large bowl. When the potatoes are done, drain and let cool. Coarsely chop the potatoes and add to the bowl. Stir gently to mix. Add the mayonnaise, mustard, celery, onion, pickle relish, dill, vinegar, garlic salt, celery seed, and salt and pepper to taste. Stir gently to mix.

Cover and chill until serving time.

Easy Back Pressure Baked Beans

Baked beans are a cookout must-have, but there's more to it than just tossing a can in a pot and stirring. A real cookout pro knows how to tune these baked beans up for exhaust notes that are just right, adding the perfect mix of spices and seasoning for flavor that'll increase your revs but take it easy on the back pressure.

Active Time: 20 minutes

Total Time: 1 hour 5 minutes

Serves: 8

2 tablespoons vegetable oil

8 ounces smoked ham hock, cubed

1 yellow onion, diced

1 red bell pepper, diced

1 serrano pepper, minced

3 cloves garlic, minced

1 tablespoon yellow mustard

2 teaspoons chile powder

1 teaspoon salt

Two 28-ounce cans baked beans

2 tablespoons molasses

¼ cup apple cider vinegar

2 tablespoons soy sauce

½ cup ketchup

Preheat the oven to 400°F.

Preheat a Dutch oven over medium heat. Add the oil and ham hock. Cook, stirring frequently, until the hock starts to brown, about 5 minutes. Add the onion, bell pepper, serrano pepper, and garlic. Cook, stirring frequently, until the vegetables are crisp-tender, about 5 minutes more.

Add the mustard, chile powder, salt, baked beans, molasses, vinegar, soy sauce, and ketchup. Bring to a simmer, stirring occasionally. Cover the Dutch oven and bake for 45 minutes.

NOS BOOST

Sometimes eating like a Toretto means getting the right fuel for a rip around the track, a pump at the gym, or twelve rounds on a punching bag. These recipes will give you the same boost a tank of NOS gives a muscle car, or help you recover from a sweat sesh properly.

Locked & Protein-Loaded Quick Bites [V, V+, GF]

If you're trying to get as big as Luke Hobbs, the not-so-secret secret is protein, and lots of it. Protein is essential post-workout, but it helps to have some in your system before you hit the weight rack, too. These quick bites and their blast of nutrients will have you chargin' hard all over the weight room.

Active Time: 25 minutes

Total Time: 25 minutes

Serves: 8

1 cup natural peanut butter or almond butter

⅔ cup coconut syrup

⅔ cup vanilla protein powder

1 cup old-fashioned oats

½ cup flaxseed meal

¼ teaspoon ground nutmeg

1 tablespoon chia seeds

2 tablespoons goji berries

2 tablespoons chopped dates

SPECIAL EQUIPMENT
Food processor

In a food processor, combine the peanut butter, coconut syrup, protein powder, oats, flaxseed meal, nutmeg, and chia seeds. Pulse to form a thick paste. Add the goji berries and dates. Pulse just until combined.

Working with wet hands, roll the mixture into 20 balls. Store in an airtight container in the refrigerator.

No-Sweat Trail Mix [V, V+, GF]

Whether prepping for the gym like Hobbs or packing school lunches for the little ones like Mia, trail mix is a tried-and-true part of any health-conscious diet. Keep your own engine revving by stashing a little trail mix in your gym bag for a post-workout recharge.

Active Time: 10 minutes

Total Time: 10 minutes

Serves: 4 to 5

½ cup goji berries

½ cup dried golden berries

½ cup roasted cashews

½ cup shelled, roasted, and salted pistachios

¼ cup dried cranberries

¼ cup dried apricots, cut into small dice

One 8-ounce bar sea-salt dark chocolate, finely chopped

In a lidded, airtight container, combine the goji berries, golden berries, cashews, pistachios, cranberries, apricots, and chocolate.

Store at room temperature.

Big-Time Beef Jerky

From Vince and Jakob to Dom and Hobbs, the Toretto clan has no shortage of well-defined action heroes. And when they get together, it can be a lot to handle, but the bonds they've formed are strong. Seasoned. Hearty. Which is a lot like this beef jerky recipe. It's a perfect pre- or post-workout snack.

Active Time:
15 minutes

Total Time:
18 hours 15 minutes

Serves:
8

2 pounds top round steak

½ cup tamari

¼ cup Worcestershire sauce

1 tablespoon brown sugar

1 teaspoon liquid smoke

1 teaspoon garlic powder

1 teaspoon onion powder

½ teaspoon ground cumin

½ teaspoon black pepper

¼ teaspoon cayenne pepper

Freeze the steak 1 hour before slicing. Then thinly slice steak into ⅛ inch strips, cutting across the grain.

In a large bowl, whisk together the tamari, Worcestershire sauce, brown sugar, liquid smoke, garlic powder, onion powder, cumin, black pepper, and cayenne. Add the steak and toss to coat. Cover and marinate in the refrigerator for 12 hours.

Preheat the oven to 180°F. Line 2 large rimmed baking pans with parchment paper.

Arrange the steak strips in a single layer, shaking off excess marinade. Bake for 4 hours or until completely dried out. Let cool completely.

Store in an airtight container in the refrigerator for up to 2 weeks.

24k Coastal Salad [V, V+, GF]

Fitness isn't always about getting big. Sometimes it's just about getting your body back in tune with itself. That doesn't always require protein loading or downing a bunch of carbs to fuel up for a workout. Sometimes it's just eating a light but satisfying meal that is full of a variety of nutrients your body needs. This healthy option is full of California notables like fresh fruit and avocado.

Active Time: 25 minutes

Total Time: 25 minutes

Serves: 4

1 medium grapefruit

½ teaspoon salt

4 cups finely chopped kale leaves, center rib removed

2 cups sliced fennel

½ cup shelled, roasted, and salted pistachios, plus more for serving

¼ cup fresh lemon juice

¼ cup water, plus more if needed

¼ cup agave nectar

3 tablespoons red wine vinegar

1 tablespoon Dijon mustard

⅓ cup extra-virgin olive oil

4 cups baby spinach

Cracked black pepper, for serving

SPECIAL EQUIPMENT
Food processor

Cut the top and bottom off the grapefruit. Set the grapefruit vertically on a cutting board and cut downward, top to bottom, to remove the peel. Over a large salad bowl, hold the peeled grapefruit and carefully cut between the segments to release them into the bowl. When all the grapefruit segments have been cut out, squeeze the remaining grapefruit juice into the bowl and discard the peel and pith. Add the salt, kale, and fennel to the bowl and toss to combine.

In a food processor or blender, combine the pistachios, lemon juice, water, agave, vinegar, and mustard. Process until smooth. While the processor is running, slowly add the olive oil. If the dressing is too thick, slowly add water until it reaches the desired consistency.

Add the spinach and dressing to the salad bowl and toss to combine. Divide among 4 salad plates. Sprinkle with black pepper and pistachios and serve.

Green Thumb Smoothie [V, V+, GF]

When you're on the go all day, it can be tough to remember to eat healthy. Once you taste this velvety, flavorful smoothie, that won't be a problem any longer—it's packed with the tastiest fruits and vegetables, plus a special blend of sweet and creamy ingredients. It's as much of a treat as it is a good-for-you shake.

Active Time:
10 minutes

Total Time:
10 minutes

Serves:
4

2 cups spinach

2 cups roughly chopped kale, stemmed, reserving 4 small leaves

1 English cucumber, chopped, reserving 4 slices

2 kiwis, peeled

1 mango, pitted, peeled, and cubed

2½ cups vanilla almond milk

1 cup gluten-free protein powder (vegetarian or vegan as needed)

1 tablespoon chia seeds, for garnish

In a blender, combine the spinach, chopped kale, cucumber, kiwis, mango, almond milk, and protein powder. Blend until smooth.

Divide among 4 glasses. Garnish each glass with a kale leaf, cucumber slice, and chia seeds.

Big Bad Dragon Fruit Smoothie [V, V+, GF]

Trying to keep up with the Torettos can wear you out, so it pays to keep the tank full. This smoothie packs a punch, with delicious dragon fruit anchoring a fresh assortment of tasty fruits. It's a nutritious and satisfying smoothie, full of flavor, with plenty of vitamins and minerals for a fighting chance at running with this crew.

Active Time:
15 minutes

Total Time:
15 minutes

Serves:
4

2½ cups dragon fruit, cubed

2 cups cubed fresh pineapple

1 cup fresh strawberries, hulled

2 ripe bananas, chopped

2 cups gluten-free oat milk

Juice and zest of 1 lime

1 cup ice cubes

In a large blender, combine the dragon fruit, pineapple, strawberries, bananas, oat milk, and lime juice, and ice, reserving a few pieces of fruit for garnish. Blend until very smooth.

Divide among 4 tall glasses. Garnish each glass with the reserved fruit and lime zest.

TIP To get all the flesh of the dragon fruit, cut it in half, then scoop flesh from the hard, inedible outer skin.

ACROSS THE GLOBE

The family's missions began in the heart of Los Angeles but they've raced around the globe. From Tokyo to Abu Dhabi, London to Brazil, they've traveled far and wide, keeping little pieces of these places with them, often in the form of a new recipe. A visit to the kitchen of any extended Toretto clan member is like an international tour of flavors and ingredients that recount their travels.

Skyscraper Kebabs [GF]

Launching a car out of one building and crashing into another is a daredevil maneuver only attempted by the most fearless rider. And that's exactly what Dom did in Dubai when the crew pulled a job at Burj Khalifa, the tallest building in the world. Consider these towering kebabs an homage to that incredible, once-in-a-lifetime move.

Active Time: 25 minutes

Total Time: 1 hour 25 minutes

Serves: 4

1 pound ground lamb

1 pound ground beef

½ cup mint leaves, roughly chopped

¼ cup cilantro leaves, roughly chopped

3 teaspoons ground coriander

2 teaspoons ginger paste

2 teaspoons paprika

1 teaspoon red pepper flakes

1 teaspoon salt

1 teaspoon black pepper

Olive oil, for brushing

Tomato wedges, for serving

Lemon wedges, for serving

SPECIAL EQUIPMENT
8 metal or wooden skewers

In a large bowl, combine the lamb, beef, mint, cilantro, coriander, ginger paste, paprika, red pepper flakes, salt, and pepper. Using wet hands, gently mix until all the ingredients are thoroughly incorporated.

Working with a handful at a time, use wet hands to form the meat mixture into ovals; thread onto skewers. Place the threaded skewers on a large baking pan as you work. When the skewers are ready, lightly cover them with plastic wrap and refrigerate for 1 hour.

Preheat a grill to medium-high. Generously brush the grates with olive oil and add the kebabs. Cook for 2 minutes, then turn. Continue to cook, turning occasionally, until all sides of the kebabs are charred and the internal temperature is 160°F, 5 to 7 minutes more. (Continue brushing the grates with oil if the kebabs start to stick.)

Serve with the tomato and lemon wedges.

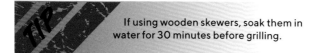

TIP

If using wooden skewers, soak them in water for 30 minutes before grilling.

First-Gear Falafel Wraps [V, V+]

Cruise into the kitchen and make these ASAP. You may think you've had falafel before, but never as good as this. Having a meat-free recipe on hand can add freshness and variety to meal-planning, and these falafel deliver: crispy, fluffy, and substantial.

Active Time: 35 minutes

Total Time: 1 hour 35 minutes

Serves: 4

FOR THE FALAFEL
One 15-ounce can chickpeas, rinsed and drained

½ cup fresh parsley, chopped

4 cloves garlic, sliced

1 shallot, diced

2 tablespoons pine nuts

2 teaspoons cumin

1 teaspoon coriander

2 teaspoons tahini

½ teaspoon paprika

¼ teaspoon salt

⅓ cup all-purpose flour

2 tablespoons olive oil

FOR THE TAHINI SAUCE
2 large cloves garlic, crushed and peeled

2 tablespoons fresh lemon juice

¼ cup tahini, plus more if needed

¼ teaspoon salt, plus more if needed

¼ teaspoon ground cumin, plus more if needed

¼ cup ice water, plus more if needed

FOR SERVING
4 pita breads, warmed, or 2 large pitas, split

1 Persian cucumber, sliced

1 cup cherry tomatoes, sliced

½ cup red onion, slivered

SPECIAL EQUIPMENT
Food processor

Fine-mesh strainer

FOR THE FALAFEL: In a food processor, combine the chickpeas, parsley, garlic, shallot, pine nuts, cumin, coriander, tahini, paprika, and salt. Pulse a few times to combine, then slowly process until a semismooth but gritty texture forms. Add the flour, a little at a time, processing after each addition, until a rough dough forms. Transfer to a medium bowl, then cover and refrigerate for 1 hour.

FOR THE TAHINI SAUCE: In a medium bowl, combine the garlic and lemon juice. Let stand 10 minutes. Remove the garlic cloves and press through a fine-mesh strainer to squeeze out as much of the flavorful liquid as possible. Discard the garlic.

Add the tahini, salt, and cumin. Whisk until blended.

Add the ice water, 1 tablespoon at a time, whisking after each addition, until smooth. If necessary, whisk in a little more water to achieve a drizzling consistency. Taste and add more salt, cumin, or lemon juice, if desired. Cover and set aside at room temperature until serving time.

Working with wet hands, form the chilled falafel mixture into 12 balls and lightly squish them down.

Heat a large skillet over medium heat and add the oil. When the oil is shimmering, fry the falafel until dark golden brown and crisp, 5 to 6 minutes, turning once.

FOR SERVING: Place 3 falafel in each pita. Top with the cucumber, tomato, red onion, and tahini sauce. Serve immediately.

Last Ride Luqaimat [V, V+]

These small bites of sweetness—a celebration treat the crew picked up after chasing the God's Eye in Abu Dhabi—are like fancy doughnut holes and are perfect for snacking. It's a good thing you can make these at home now because they go down easy and will have you reaching for the "last one" every time a batch is baked.

Active Time:	Total Time:	Serves:
30 minutes	1 hour	4

1 cup all-purpose flour

1 teaspoon active dry yeast

1 tablespoon granulated sugar

1 teaspoon cornstarch

1 teaspoon vegetable oil

¼ teaspoon salt

¼ teaspoon cardamom

½ cup lukewarm water, plus more if needed

½ teaspoon orange blossom water

Vegetable oil, for frying

¼ cup date syrup, for serving

¼ cup chocolate hazelnut spread, warmed for serving

In a medium bowl, whisk together the flour, yeast, sugar, cornstarch, vegetable oil, salt, and cardamom. In a small bowl, combine the lukewarm water and orange blossom water. Slowly add the water to the dry ingredients, mixing with wet hands, until a sticky dough forms. If needed, add additional water. Cover and let stand at room temperature for 30 minutes.

Fill a deep skillet with 2 inches of oil. Heat over medium heat to 350°F. Transfer the dough to a large zip-top bag. Fill a glass with water to wet scissors occasionally. Cut the edge from the bag about ¾ inch across. Squeeze dollops of batter into the hot oil, wetting the scissors occasionally to prevent the batter from sticking. Do not overfill the pan.

Fry the luqaimat until golden brown, about 4 minutes, using a slotted spoon to roll and turn as they fry. Transfer to a paper towel–lined plate.

Serve warm, drizzled with the date syrup and chocolate hazelnut spread.

Four-Wheel-Drive Dosas [V]

With so many miles logged with the crew, it's hard to remember where or when something gets added into the mix. Take dosas, a versatile, savory crepe-like street food known for their unique, slightly sour flavor. Typically eaten with breakfast but with a range that stretches from snack to full meal, this is the all-wheel-drive of your menu—perfect anytime, anyplace.

Active Time: 1 hour

Total Time: 1 hour

Serves: 4

1 Yukon Gold potato, peeled

1 cup cauliflower florets, chopped

¼ cup chickpea flour

¼ cup lentil flour

¼ cup rice flour

¼ cup whole wheat flour

½ teaspoon salt, divided

1½ cups water

2 tablespoons vegetable oil, plus more for frying the dosas

1 teaspoon yellow mustard seed

½ teaspoon black mustard seed

1 shallot, slivered

½ cup diced red bell peppers

½ teaspoon ground ginger

1 tablespoon fresh lemon juice

½ cup cilantro, chopped

Chile sauce, for serving

Greek yogurt, for serving

Place the potato in a medium pot and add enough water to cover. Bring to a boil over high heat. Reduce the heat to medium-high and cook until fork-tender, about 12 minutes. Remove the potato and add the cauliflower to the pot. Cook for 3 minutes, then drain. Cool and roughly chop the potato; set both vegetables aside.

In a medium bowl, combine the chickpea flour, lentil flour, rice flour, whole wheat flour, ¼ teaspoon of the salt, and the water. Whisk to combine.

Heat a large nonstick or cast-iron skillet over medium heat. Add a small amount of oil, about ¼ teaspoon, and spread with a paper towel. Pour a generous ½ cup of the batter into the pan, swirling to spread thin. Fry the dosa until the edges are crisp, about 3 minutes. Remove to a large plate. Repeat with the remaining batter, stacking the dosas as you work (you should get 4 dosas).

In the same skillet, add the 2 tablespoons oil. Turn the heat to high. Add the yellow and black mustard seeds. Cook, stirring, until they begin to pop, about 1 minute. Add the shallot. Cook, stirring occasionally, until tender, about 1 to 2 minutes. Add the bell pepper and cook, stirring occasionally, until crisp-tender, 2 to 3 minutes. Add the cooked potato and cauliflower, the remaining ¼ teaspoon salt, and the ground ginger. Cook, stirring occasionally, until the vegetables are tender and lightly browned, 3 to 4 minutes. Stir in the lemon juice and cilantro.

Divide the filling among the dosas and serve immediately with the chile sauce and yogurt.

Quarter Mile Manakish [V]

Doughy, saucy, and spicy, this is the sort of dish that could easily be inhaled, so just try to eat this manakish one bite at a time.

Active Time: 🥄
20 minutes

Total Time: 🥄
1 hour 10 minutes

Serves: 🥄
4

½ cup warm water

1 teaspoon granulated sugar

1½ teaspoons active dry yeast

1¼ cups plus 2 tablespoons all-purpose flour, plus more for dusting

1 teaspoon dried oregano

4 tablespoons olive oil, divided

¾ teaspoon salt, divided

3 tablespoons za'atar

8 ounces mozzarella cheese, shredded

4 ounces feta cheese, crumbled

1 teaspoon caraway seeds

½ teaspoon cumin seeds

1 cup Greek yogurt

2 teaspoons ground sumac

1 teaspoon black pepper

1 tomato, seeded and diced

Fresh mint, for garnish

In a large bowl, stir together the warm water and sugar. Sprinkle the yeast over the warm water. Stir and let stand until foamy, about 5 minutes.

Add the 1¼ cups flour to the bowl. Stir until well combined. Cover and let rest for 10 minutes. Add the 2 tablespoons flour, the oregano, 2 tablespoons olive oil, and ½ teaspoon salt. Stir until well combined and a rough dough ball comes together. Cover and let rest for 30 minutes.

Combine the remaining 2 tablespoons oil and the za'atar; set aside.

Preheat the oven to 375°F. Line a large rimmed baking pan with parchment paper.

Lightly flour a work surface. Divide the dough into 4 portions and roll each out thin. Transfer to the prepared pan.

In a medium bowl, combine the mozzarella and feta cheeses. Drizzle the seasoned oil over the dough circles. Sprinkle with the cheese, caraway seeds, and cumin seeds. Bake for 20 minutes or until golden brown.

While the flatbreads are baking, stir together the yogurt, sumac, black pepper, remaining ¼ teaspoon salt, and the tomato in a bowl.

Garnish the flatbreads with fresh mint. Serve with the tomato-yogurt mixture.

Welcome to Tokyo Takoyaki

Different cars, different stores, and different foods! Traveling to new places brings new experiences, and for the uninitiated, Japan's street food scene may be overwhelming. There are so many choices, but you really don't want to miss the fried octopus. One bite and you'll be planning how to cook it for your next get-together.

Active Time: 35 minutes

Total Time: 35 minutes

Serves: 4

1 large egg

1 cup water

2 teaspoons soy sauce

¾ teaspoon dashi powder

¾ cup all-purpose flour

1 tablespoon vegetable oil

½ bunch scallions, sliced

3 tablespoons beni shoga (chopped pickled red ginger)

2 tablespoons crispy rice cereal

6 ounces cooked octopus, cut into bite-size pieces

Kewpie mayonnaise, for garnish

Katsu sauce, for garnish

Sliced scallions, for garnish

Pickled red ginger, for garnish

SPECIAL EQUIPMENT
16-hole takoyaki pan or cake pop pan

Wooden skewer

In a medium bowl, whisk together the egg, water, soy sauce, dashi powder, and flour. Pour into a cup with a spout, such as a glass measuring cup.

Heat a 16-hole takoyaki pan or cake pop pan over medium-high heat. Add a little bit of the oil to each hole. Use a paper towel to evenly rub the oil around each hole and over the flat surface of the pan.

When the oil begins to smoke, reduce the heat to medium. Distribute the batter evenly among the holes. (It will overflow a little bit; that's okay.) Quickly sprinkle the sliced scallions, chopped pickled ginger, and crispy rice cereal over the batter. Add 2 pieces of cooked octopus to each hole.

Using a wooden skewer, cut straight lines through the batter to create squares around the holes. Using the skewer, roll the balls downward 90 degrees, carefully tucking the points of the squares underneath each ball with the skewer. Cook until golden brown and lightly crisp, 5 to 7 minutes.

Arrange the takoyaki on a platter. Drizzle with the mayonnaise and katsu sauce. Sprinkle with more sliced scallions and pickled ginger. Serve immediately.

Clutch Okonomiyaki

Throw your next gathering into a higher gear with this okonomiyaki recipe. Similar to a pancake or frittata, and topped with an assortment of ingredients, it's a Japanese street food classic. Sometimes translated as "as-you-like-it pancake," this dish is more savory than most flapjacks due to its seafood or meat filling.

Active Time: 35 minutes

Total Time: 35 minutes

Serves: 4

FOR THE PANCAKES
4 cups shredded cabbage

½ bunch scallions, sliced

2 tablespoons chopped pickled ginger

½ teaspoon salt

1 cup water

1 teaspoon dashi powder

1 cup all-purpose flour, plus more for dusting

½ teaspoon baking powder

4 large eggs

2 tablespoons vegetable oil

6 strips bacon, halved

FOR THE SAUCE
¼ cup ketchup

2 tablespoons date syrup

2 tablespoons Worcestershire sauce

2 tablespoons (12g) brown sugar

FOR SERVING
Kewpie mayonnaise

Sliced scallions

Bonito flakes

Togarashi seasoning

FOR THE PANCAKES: In a large bowl, combine the cabbage, scallions, pickled ginger, and salt. Use your hands to mix until well combined.

In a medium bowl, whisk together the water and dashi powder. Whisk in 1 cup flour, the baking powder, and eggs. Pour over the cabbage mixture and stir to thoroughly combine.

Heat a cast-iron griddle over medium heat. Spread the oil over the griddle. Divide the cabbage mixture into 4 piles and gently spread them out until about 1 inch tall, using a spatula to form them into circles. Place a little bit of flour in a fine-mesh strainer and lightly dust the tops of the pancakes with flour. Use a spatula to form into circles. Arrange 3 pieces of bacon on top of each pancake.

Cook the pancakes for about 5 minutes, then carefully turn. Cook for 5 minutes more, then turn again. Cook 3 minutes more, turn, then cook for 3 minutes more.

FOR THE SAUCE: In a small bowl, combine the ketchup, date syrup, Worcestershire sauce, and brown sugar.

FOR SERVING: Divide the pancakes among 4 plates. Brush liberally with the sauce. Drizzle with the mayonnaise, and garnish with the scallions, bonito flakes, ginger, and togarashi.

Japanese-Style Fruit Jelly [V, V+, GF]

Spend time in a new place, and there's a tendency to pick up the local customs and tastes. Case in point with these tasty little jelly treats. A far cry from the kind of jelly you've been spreading on your PB&J sandwiches, these molded sweets make a great snack when you want a snack as unique as your ride.

Active Time: **Total Time:**   **Serves:**

25 minutes   1 hour 35 minutes   12

3 cups water

5 tablespoons agar-agar powder

¼ cup granulated sugar

One 8.5-ounce can mandarin oranges in fruit juice, drained and juice from the can reserved

5 strawberries, stemmed and halved

½ cup blackberries

SPECIAL EQUIPMENT
2- to 6-cavity, large, domed silicone mold

Wooden skewer

In a medium pot, bring the water and agar-agar to a boil over medium-high heat, whisking to dissolve the agar-agar. When the liquid comes to a boil, reduce heat to low. Add the sugar and the juice from the can of mandarin oranges. Continue cooking for about 3 minutes, whisking constantly to dissolve the sugar.

Pour about ½ inch of the liquid into each cavity of a 2- to 6-cavity (12 total), large, domed silicone mold. Pop any bubbles with a wooden skewer, then refrigerate just until lightly set, about 10 minutes.

Arrange the fruits on the thin layers of jelly, then pour the remaining liquid over the top (reheat if it is no longer pourable). Pop any bubbles and return to the refrigerator until completely set, at least 1 hour.

When ready to serve, carefully turn out the jellies onto a serving platter or plates.

Drift King Ramen

On the streets of Tokyo, the Drift King runs the racing scene, but ramen rules the restaurant world. You can't walk a city block without passing a ramen joint—or a racer in a souped-up car.

Active Time: 20 minutes

Total Time: 50 minutes

Serves: 4

10 cups vegetable broth

¼ cup tamari sauce

1 tablespoon toasted sesame oil

1 tablespoon garlic paste

1 tablespoon minced ginger

1 tablespoon fish sauce

2 teaspoons bonito soup stock (such as HONDASHI®)

2 teaspoons red miso paste

2 teaspoons sriracha

½ teaspoon ground cinnamon

4 large eggs

Four 3-ounce packages ramen noodles, seasoning omitted

1 cup mushrooms

1 cup matchstick-cut carrots

2 jalapeños, sliced thin

½ cup frozen corn kernels, thawed

½ cup frozen peas, thawed

Scallions, sliced on the bias, for garnish

Chile paste, for garnish

Toasted sesame seeds, for garnish

Nori strips, for garnish

In a large pot, combine the vegetable broth, tamari, sesame oil, garlic paste, minced garlic, fish sauce, dashi, miso, sriracha, and cinnamon. Whisk to combine, then bring to a boil over medium heat. When the broth is boiling, reduce the heat and simmer for 15 minutes.

While the broth simmers, bring a medium pot of water to a boil. Add the eggs and cook for 7 minutes. Remove from the pan with a slotted spoon and place in a bowl of ice water. When the eggs are cool, peel them.

When the broth has simmered for 15 minutes, add the noodles and cook for 3 minutes. Drain the noodles through a strainer into a large bowl. Divide the noodles among 4 large bowls. Pour hot broth over the noodles. Cut the eggs in half lengthwise and add 2 halves to each bowl. Top the bowls with mushrooms, carrots, jalapeños, corn, and peas.

Garnish with the scallions, chile paste, sesame seeds, and nori. Serve immediately.

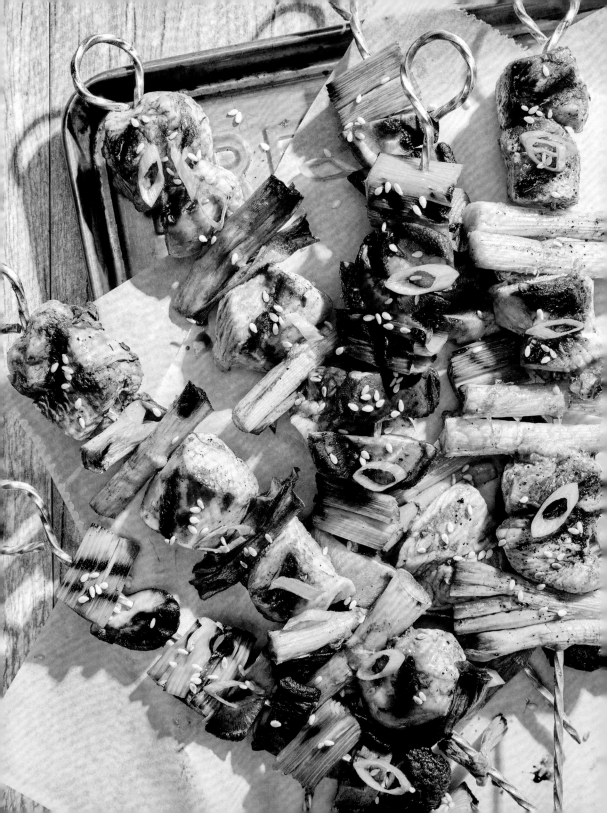

Copilot Yakitori

Packing grilled, flavorful chicken with a mix of smoky sweetness, this yakitori is as easily a sit-down meal as on the go. Easy to make and super portable, this yakitori recipe is exactly the sort of dish you want within easy reach in the passenger's seat—literally.

Active Time: 35 minutes

Total Time: 35 minutes

Serves: 4

1 pound boneless, skinless chicken thighs, cut into 1-inch pieces

1 bunch scallions, cut into 1-inch pieces

1 leek, trimmed and cut into 12 slices (white and light green parts), rinsed and patted dry

16 shiitake mushrooms, stemmed

¾ cup soy sauce

1 tablespoon mirin

1 tablespoon fish sauce

1 tablespoon sake

1 tablespoon water

Scallions, sliced on the bias, for garnish

Toasted sesame seeds, for garnish

SPECIAL EQUIPMENT
8 wooden or metal skewers

If using wooden skewers, soak 8 in water for 30 minutes before grilling.

Thread the chicken and scallions on 4 skewers. Arrange the leek pieces on a microwave-safe plate and microwave on high for 20 seconds to soften. Thread the leeks and mushroom caps on the 4 remaining skewers.

In a small bowl, stir together the soy sauce, mirin, fish sauce, sake, and water; set aside.

Heat a large griddle-length grill pan over medium-high heat. Lightly spray the skewers and grill pan with nonstick spray.

Cook the skewers until the vegetables are charred and the chicken is cooked through, about 10 to 15 minutes, turning occasionally. During the last 5 to 7 minutes, brush the skewers with the soy mixture after each turn.

Divide the chicken-scallion skewers and leek-mushroom skewers among 4 plates. Sprinkle with the scallions and sesame seeds.

Late-Night Yakisoba

Putting in work behind the wheel can empty the tank and lower your energy levels. There's a certain kind of dish you just want to dig into after a late night out on the road—savory, tangy, rich. This yakisoba is a dish that will fill you up and end your night on a good note.

Active Time: 20 minutes

Total Time: 20 minutes

Serves: 4

3 teaspoons vegetable oil, divided

1 yellow, red, or orange bell pepper, stemmed, seeded, and sliced

1 carrot, peeled and thinly sliced

1 small white onion, cut into thick slivers

2 cups shredded napa cabbage

1 medium zucchini, cut into half-moons

1 bunch scallions, whites cut into 1-inch pieces, greens sliced, divided

1 pound chicken breast, thinly sliced

One 16-ounce package fresh yakisoba noodles

½ cup ketchup

½ cup hoisin sauce

¼ cup mirin

2 tablespoons Worcestershire sauce

In an extra-large skillet, heat 1 teaspoon oil over medium-high heat. Add the bell pepper, carrot, onion, cabbage, zucchini, and scallion whites to the pan. Toss to coat, then cook for 2 minutes without stirring. Toss and cook for 2 to 3 minutes more. Remove from the pan to a large bowl.

Add 1 more teaspoon oil to the pan, then add the chicken. Toss to coat, then cook for 2 minutes without stirring. Toss and cook for 2 to 3 minutes more. Remove to the bowl with the vegetables.

Add the remaining 1 teaspoon oil to the pan, then the yakisoba noodles. Spread the noodles out over the pan and let cook for 1 minute without stirring. When the noodles begin to char, add the chicken and vegetables to the pan. Add the ketchup, hoisin, mirin, and Worcestershire sauce. Cook, stirring frequently, until everything is well combined and nice and hot, about 2 minutes.

Divide among 4 plates. Top with the scallion greens and serve.

Five-Star Yuca Fries [V, V+, GF]

You may think you've already eaten the best fries of your life, but you're wrong. These Brazilian yuca fries are full of unique spice and flavor like nothing you've tried before. Once you've had them, you'll never want to eat fries any other way.

Active Time: 25 minutes

Total Time: 40 minutes

Serves: 4

2 quarts water

1½ teaspoons salt, plus more for sprinkling

2 pounds yuca root (also called cassava)

Vegetable oil, for frying

Black pepper

Paprika, for seasoning

Ketchup, for dipping

In a medium pot, bring the water and 1½ teaspoons salt to a boil.

While the water heats, cut the ends from the yuca. Carefully cut the yuca into 3- to 4-inch sections. Use the tip of a sharp knife to slice vertically through the skin, about ¼ inch deep. Gently lift up the skin with the tip of a knife to remove it; discard the skin. Cut the yuca sections into ½-inch slices, then lay flat and cut into ½-inch sticks.

Add the yuca to the boiling water, then remove from the heat. Stir and let stand for 15 minutes. Drain and pat very dry with paper towels.

In a Dutch oven, heat 3 inches vegetable oil to 350°F. Fry the yuca pieces in batches, turning often, until golden brown, about 5 minutes per batch, allowing the oil to come back up to temperature between batches. Drain on a paper towel–lined baking pan.

Sprinkle with salt, black pepper, and paprika while hot. Serve with ketchup.

California Cachorro Quente

Ask an Angeleno where the best hot dogs in the world are and they'll tell you to pick any vendor on the streets of LA after a night out with your friends. Still, even LA natives would have trouble denying the seasoned and charred greatness of a Cachorro Quente.

Active Time: 30 minutes

Total Time: 45 minutes

Serves: 4

1 tablespoon butter

1 small white onion, cut into medium dice

1 green bell pepper, stemmed, seeded, and cut into medium dice

1 jalapeño, sliced, plus more diced jalapeños, for topping

2 garlic cloves, minced

1 cup tomato sauce

½ cup water

½ teaspoon salt

½ teaspoon dried thyme

½ teaspoon dried oregano

¼ teaspoon black pepper

4 all-beef hot dogs

4 hot dog buns

Mayonnaise, for topping

Mustard, for topping

Ketchup, for topping

Shoestring potatoes, for topping

In a large skillet, melt the butter over medium heat. Add the onion, bell pepper, sliced jalapeño, and garlic, and cook, stirring frequently, until the vegetables soften slightly, about 4 minutes. Add the tomato sauce, water, salt, thyme, oregano, and black pepper. Cook, stirring occasionally, for 10 minutes.

Use a small sharp knife to cut into the hot dogs vertically, about halfway through. Add the hot dogs to the vegetable mixture. Cook for 10 minutes more, stirring occasionally.

Divide half of the vegetable mixture among 4 buns. Add the hot dogs, then top with the remaining vegetable mixture.

Top with mayonnaise, mustard, ketchup, shoestring potatoes, and diced jalapeños as desired.

Fuel-Up Kibe

Adventures in Brazil brought some delectable new flavors into the family kitchen. And for good reason, because kibe will sneak up on you. It's a tiny dish that packs a powerful punch, way bigger than you'd expect. It's the sort of attitude the family embodies.

Active Time: 50 minutes

Total Time: 5 hours 20 minutes

Serves: 8

1 cup bulgur wheat

2 cups beef broth

1 tablespoon vegetable oil, plus more for frying

1 large onion, cut into small dice

½ cup chopped pine nuts

1 tablespoon garlic paste

½ teaspoon ground cinnamon

¼ teaspoon ground mace

1 pound ground beef

1 pound ground lamb

½ cup chopped fresh parsley

1 teaspoon salt

1 teaspoon black pepper

1 teaspoon ground sumac

½ cup packed mint leaves

Lime wedges, for garnish

Tahini, for garnish

Mint leaves, for garnish

SPECIAL EQUIPMENT
Food processor

Place the bulgur in a medium bowl. In a small pot, bring the broth to a boil over high heat. Boil for 3 minutes, then pour the water over the bulgur. Cover and set aside for 30 minutes.

In an extra-large skillet over medium heat, heat 1 tablespoon oil. Add half of the onion, the pine nuts, garlic paste, cinnamon, and mace. Cook, stirring frequently, until very fragrant and the onion is softened, about 2 minutes. Add half each of the ground beef and ground lamb. Cook, using a wooden spoon to break up the meat, until cooked through, 6 to 8 minutes. Stir in the parsley and ½ teaspoon each of the salt and pepper. Transfer the mixture to a bowl.

Drain the bulgur, gently pressing to remove any remaining liquid. Place in a food processor. Add the remaining beef and lamb, remaining ½ teaspoon each salt and pepper, the sumac, and the ½ cup mint leaves. Process until smooth. Transfer to a second bowl. Cover both bowls and chill in the refrigerator for 4 hours.

Working with wet hands, form the bulgur mixture into golf ball-size balls. Gently push your finger into each ball, working the mixture around your finger to form a cone shape. Stuff about 1 tablespoon of the meat mixture in the hole. Pinch to seal and shape it into an oval. Repeat with remaining bulgur and meat mixtures.

In a Dutch oven, heat 2 inches of oil to 350°F. Working in batches, gently add the kibe to the hot oil and fry, turning occasionally, until dark brown and crisp, 4 to 5 minutes per batch, allowing the oil to come back up to temperature between batches. Keep the kibe warm in a 200°F oven while you cook the rest.

Arrange the kibe on a serving platter. Garnish with the mint leaves, lime wedges, and tahini.

X-Treme X-Tudos

When you've had your fill of fast food, give this signature Brazilian dish a shot. So much more than a burger, X-tudos are a meal on a bun, with egg and ham in addition to the ground beef patty and out-of-the-ordinary spices. After experiencing one of these unique sandwiches, there may be no going back to an ordinary burger again.

Active Time:	Total Time:	Serves:
30 minutes	30 minutes	4

1½ pounds ground chuck	1 teaspoon butter	¼ cup cooked corn
1 teaspoon salt	4 large eggs	Four ½-inch tomato slices
½ teaspoon black pepper	4 slices cheddar cheese	4 thick slices deli ham
½ garlic powder	¼ cup mayonnaise	½ cup shoestring potatoes
¼ teaspoon ground cumin	4 hamburger buns	Ketchup, for serving
6 strips bacon, halved	8 leaves Bibb lettuce	Mustard, for serving

In a large bowl, combine the ground chuck, salt, pepper, garlic powder, and ground cumin. Gently work with your hands to combine the ingredients, being careful not to overwork the mixture. Form the mixture into 4 bun-width patties.

Heat a large cast-iron skillet over medium heat. Add the bacon and cook until crisp, turning often, 6 to 8 minutes. Remove from the skillet. Add the butter, then crack the eggs into skillet. Cook for about 2 minutes, then turn and cook 1 minute more. Remove from the skillet.

Add the patties and cook for 4 minutes. Turn and cook 3 minutes more. Add the cheese and cook for 1 minute more. Remove the patties from skillet.

Spread mayo evenly over all the buns' cut sides. Divide the lettuce, corn, and tomato slices among the bottom buns. Add the patties, ham slices, fried eggs, and shoestring potatoes. Top with the top buns. Serve with ketchup and mustard.

Forever Loyal Pastel de Queijo [V]

Pasteles de Queijos are reliably satiating handheld pastries that go over great with anyone looking for a light but flavorful snack that packs more punch than it shows.

Active Time: 1 hour 10 minutes

Total Time: 1 hour 55 minutes

Serves: 10

4 cups all-purpose flour, plus more for dusting

1 tablespoon salt

2 tablespoons cornstarch

1½ teaspoons baking soda

1 teaspoon granulated sugar

¼ teaspoon cayenne pepper

2 tablespoons vegetable oil

½ cup warm water

½ cup warm milk

4 large whole eggs, plus 1 beaten egg, for sealing

½ cup shredded cheddar cheese

½ cup shredded Oaxaca cheese

1½ teaspoons guajillo chile flakes

Vegetable oil, for frying

Powdered sugar, for garnish

In a large bowl, whisk together the flour, salt, cornstarch, baking soda, sugar, and cayenne. Add the oil and whisk to combine. Add the warm water and milk and stir to combine. Add the 4 whole eggs, one at a time, stirring vigorously after each addition, until a dough ball forms.

Lightly dust a work surface with flour. Knead the dough on the work surface until smooth, about 8 minutes. Dust the dough ball with flour. Place in the bowl and let rest, covered, for 45 minutes.

Divide the dough into 20 balls. Roll each ball into a circle a little larger than 3½ inches in diameter. Use a 5-inch biscuit cutter to cut a perfect circle. Discard the excess dough, and repeat with remaining dough circles.

Divide the cheddar cheese, Oaxaca cheese, and chile flakes evenly among the dough circles. Brush the beaten egg along the edges of the dough circles and fold over the filling, pressing to seal with your fingers.

In a Dutch oven, heat 2 inches of oil to 350°F. Working in batches, fry the pastries, turning occasionally, until golden, about 5 minutes, allowing the oil to come back up to temperature between each batch. Transfer the cooked pastries to a paper towel–lined baking pan to drain. Arrange the pastries on a serving platter. Dust with powdered sugar and serve warm.

Family-First Fritters [V, GF]

Mix up your meat and potato routine with a batch of these tasty malanga fritters. These delicacies are a quick-prep recipe packed with a ton of unique spice and flavor that speak to the recipe's rich history. Next time you cook for the family, think of these first. They may just become your clutch meal.

Active Time: 20 minutes   **Total Time:** 20 minutes   **Serves:** 6

½ cup mayonnaise

3 tablespoons chile sauce

2 tablespoons garlic paste

1 pound taro root, peeled

2 teaspoons adobo seasoning

1 clove garlic, minced

1 cup parsley, chopped

½ teaspoon ground coriander

½ teaspoon black pepper

2 large eggs, beaten

Vegetable oil, for frying

Salt

In a small bowl, stir together the mayonnaise, chile sauce, and garlic paste. Set aside.

Grate the taro root on a box grater. Place the grated taro in a clean kitchen towel and roll it up. Squeeze the towel over the sink to remove as much excess moisture as you can.

In a large bowl, combine the grated taro, adobo seasoning, garlic, parsley, coriander, and pepper. Add the eggs and mix well to incorporate all the ingredients.

In a Dutch oven, heat 2½ inches of oil to 325°F. Drop spoonfuls of the taro mixture into the oil and fry, turning occasionally, until crispy and golden brown, 5 to 7 minutes. Transfer the cooked fritters to a paper towel–lined baking pan to drain. Salt to taste while still hot.

Serve the fritters with the dipping sauce.

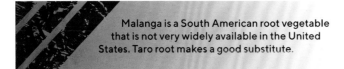

Malanga is a South American root vegetable that is not very widely available in the United States. Taro root makes a good substitute.

Pub-Style Scotch Eggs

Most of the time when the family is in London, they're experiencing the city from behind the wheel of a car. Still, you've gotta stop for a pint now and then. Scotch eggs are a classic in households, restaurants, and pubs alike across the UK.

Active Time: 35 minutes

Total Time: 1 hour

Serves: 8

8 ounces ground pork	1 teaspoon granulated garlic	3 large eggs, beaten
1 teaspoon ground thyme	1 teaspoon salt	2 cups soft breadcrumbs
1 teaspoon ground sage	1 teaspoon black pepper	Vegetable oil, for frying
1 teaspoon ground rosemary	8 large eggs	Hot or honey mustard, for serving (optional)
1 teaspoon ground nutmeg	1½ cups all-purpose flour	

Fill a large pot halfway with water and bring to a boil over high heat.

While the water comes to a boil, in a large bowl, combine the pork, thyme, sage, rosemary, nutmeg, garlic, salt, and black pepper. Use your hands to gently mix until all the ingredients are well combined.

When the water is boiling, carefully add the eggs to the pot. Cook for 6 minutes. After 6 minutes, remove from the heat. Transfer the eggs with a slotted spoon to a bowl of ice water. When the eggs are cool, peel them.

Divide the sausage into 8 even portions and flatten them into large patties. Place 1 egg on each patty. Gently roll the sausage around the egg, ensuring the sausage is in direct contact with the egg and completely sealed. Roll the sausage-wrapped eggs in the flour, then in the beaten egg, and finally in the breadcrumbs to coat.

In a Dutch oven, heat 3 inches of oil to 350°F. Fry half of the eggs in hot oil until browned and crisp, turning often, about 5 minutes. Transfer to a paper towel-lined plate to drain. Repeat with the remaining eggs.

Serve with mustard, if desired.

Classic Bangers & Mash [GF]

Bangers and mash are about as British as can be. And for good reason—it's hard to find fault with a plate of hearty sausage and creamy potatoes. The mix of culinary history and classic textures ensure that when the Toretto crew crosses the pond, a plate of these is sure to end up on the table.

Active Time: 45 minutes

Total Time: 45 minutes

Serves: 8

6 Yukon Gold potatoes, cut into large chunks

2 teaspoons vegetable oil

8 English-style sausages

4 ounces smoked pork belly, diced

5 tablespoons butter

1½ cups whole milk

1 large onion, slivered

2 tablespoons white vinegar

2 tablespoons all-purpose flour

1½ cups beef broth

1 teaspoon fresh thyme leaves

1 medium shallot, diced

1½ cups frozen peas, thawed

Salt

Black pepper

Bring a large pot of salted water to a boil. Add the potatoes and boil until fork-tender, about 12 minutes.

While the potatoes come to a boil, heat a large skillet over medium-high heat. Add the oil and sausages and cook, turning often, until browned and cooked through, about 8 minutes. Remove to a plate.

Drain the potatoes and return the pot to medium heat. Add the pork belly and cook, stirring occasionally, until the fat begins to render and the pork begins to brown, about 5 minutes. Return the potatoes to the pot, along with 2 tablespoons butter and the milk. Use a potato masher to mash. Season to taste with salt and pepper. Keep warm.

In the same pan the sausages were cooked in, cook the onion over medium heat, stirring often, until lightly browned, about 10 minutes. Add the vinegar, scraping the bottom of the pan with a wooden spoon to loosen any browned bits. Add 2 tablespoons butter and the flour. Whisk to combine, then add the beef broth and bring to a simmer. Simmer, stirring frequently, until thickened, about 5 minutes. Stir in the thyme leaves. Transfer to a serving dish.

In the same pan the gravy was made in, cook the shallot until fragrant, 1 to 2 minutes. Add the remaining 1 tablespoon butter and the peas. Cook, stirring, until peas are tender, 3 to 4 minutes. Season to taste with salt and pepper, and gently mash with a fork.

Serve the sausages on the mashed potatoes, covered in gravy, with buttered peas on the side.

Bespoke Bourguignonne Burger

Consider this tender burger that's as well adorned as Deckard Shaw in one of his luxury cars and bespoke suits the next time the situation calls for hearty, comfort food with an elevated flair.

Active Time: 35 minutes

Total Time: 35 minutes

Serves: 4

1½ pounds ground chuck

1 teaspoon salt

1 teaspoon black pepper

1 tablespoon vegetable oil

3 tablespoons butter

¾ cup red onion, diced

8 ounces button mushrooms, trimmed and sliced

½ cup dry red wine

2 teaspoons fresh thyme leaves

¾ teaspoon herbes de Provence

4 slices white cheddar

4 brioche buns

¼ cup crème fraîche

2 teaspoons white wine vinegar

1½ tablespoons horseradish

4 leaves leaf lettuce

8 thin slices tomato

1 tablespoon chopped chives, for garnish

Steak sauce, for serving (optional)

Divide the ground chuck into 4 pieces and form them into patties. Season with salt and pepper and brush with the oil; set aside.

Preheat the grill to medium.

Heat a large skillet over medium heat. Add 1 tablespoon butter and the onion. Cook, stirring frequently, for 5 minutes. Add the mushrooms and cook, stirring often, 5 minutes more. Add the wine, scraping the bottom of the pan with a wooden spoon to loosen any browned bits. Cook for 5 minutes more to reduce the wine a bit. Add the remaining 2 tablespoons butter, the thyme, and herbes de Provence. Stir to combine and remove from the heat.

Grill the patties for 4 minutes, then turn and grill for 4 minutes more. Add a slice of cheese to each patty and cook for 1 minute more or until melted. Lightly toast the buns on the grill.

In a small bowl, stir together the crème fraîche, vinegar, and horseradish.

Top the bottom buns with lettuce, tomato, beef patties, mushrooms, and horseradish sauce. Garnish with fresh chives, then top with the top buns. Serve with steak sauce, if desired.

Sideswipe Shawarma

London's street food scene is one of the best in the world, with an incredibly diverse array of quick bites and hearty meals found on nearly every corner. If you're ever in town and find yourself overwhelmed by the options, you can't go wrong with shawarma. If you don't have a trip to the UK planned any time soon, this recipe will tide you over.

Active Time: 30 minutes

Total Time: 6 hours 30 minutes

Serves: 4

FOR THE CHICKEN
1 tablespoon ground coriander

2 teaspoons ground cumin

2 teaspoons turmeric

2 teaspoons smoked paprika

1 teaspoon garlic salt

1 teaspoon black pepper

1½ pounds boneless, skinless chicken thighs

3 tablespoons fresh lemon juice

2 tablespoons olive oil

Olive oil cooking spray, for greasing the grill

FOR THE SAUCE
1 cup Greek yogurt

1 tablespoon garlic paste

1 teaspoon cumin seeds

¼ teaspoon cayenne pepper

FOR SERVING
2 cups loosely packed arugula

½ red onion, slivered

1 tomato, halved and sliced

4 pitas, warmed

Crumbled feta (optional)

Hot sauce (optional)

FOR THE CHICKEN: In a small bowl, combine the coriander, cumin, turmeric, paprika, garlic salt, and pepper. Place the chicken in a gallon-size zip-top bag. Add the spice mixture, lemon juice, and olive oil. Seal and massage the bag thoroughly to coat everything. Place the bag in a bowl and refrigerate for 6 hours.

Spray the grill grates with cooking spray, then preheat the grill to medium-high. Grill the chicken until lightly charred and the interior reaches 165°F, turning once. Let rest for 5 minutes, then slice the chicken ½ inch thick.

FOR THE SAUCE: While chicken rests, in a small bowl, stir together the yogurt, garlic paste, cumin seeds, and cayenne.

FOR SERVING: Divide the arugula, chicken, sauce, onion, and tomato among the 4 pitas. Serve with the feta and hot sauce, if desired.

Are You Ready Rib Eye [GF]

Sometimes things don't go according to plan, even with Mr. Nobody and his team backing up the Torettos. But with some simple, straightforward grill work, you'll have a tender, juicy steak worthy of Deckard's last meal. This recipe brings the best out of a cut of beef in a way that would surely have him sending compliments to the chef.

Active Time: 20 minutes

Total Time: 30 minutes

Serves: 4

1 tablespoon fennel seeds

1 tablespoon paprika

1 tablespoon smoked salt

1 tablespoon brown sugar

2 teaspoons black pepper

Four 12-ounce rib eye steaks

2 tablespoons vegetable oil

½ cup softened butter

¼ cup Stilton cheese

1 tablespoon fresh thyme leaves

1 tablespoon chopped fresh tarragon

Mashed potatoes, for serving (optional)

Red wine, for serving (optional)

SPECIAL EQUIPMENT
Electric hand mixer with a whisk attachment

Preheat the grill to medium-high.

In a small bowl, combine the fennel seeds, paprika, smoked salt, brown sugar, and pepper. Place the steaks on a large rimmed baking pan. Sprinkle the spice rub on all sides of the steaks, pressing in with the palm of your hand. Drizzle with the oil and rub with your hands. Press the steak on the pan to collect any residual seasoning. Let rest for 10 minutes.

While the steak rests, in a medium bowl with an electric hand mixer fitted with the whisk attachment, whip the butter until light and fluffy, about 5 minutes. Add the Stilton cheese, thyme, and tarragon. Beat on low, scraping down the sides of the bowl, until well combined, about 1 minute; set aside.

Grill the steaks about 3 minutes per side. Rotate 90 degrees and grill 2 more minutes per side for medium-rare (130°F to 140°F).

Top each steak with a dollop of the prepared butter. Serve with mashed potatoes and red wine, if desired.

Custom-Built Pretzels [V]

Food carts have been a part of the NYC landscape since long before the food truck craze went global. And one of the most OG street foods of all time is the New York pretzel. Warm and salty, its unmistakable aroma will have you hooked from a block away.

Active Time: 40 minutes

Total Time: 1 hour 25 minutes

Serves: 8

1½ cups warm water

2 teaspoons active dry yeast

2 tablespoons granulated sugar

1½ teaspoons salt

2½ tablespoons melted butter, plus more for brushing

4 cups all-purpose flour, plus more for dusting

3 quarts water

⅔ cup baking soda

2 large eggs, beaten

Coarse salt

Mustard, for serving

SPECIAL EQUIPMENT
Electric mixer with a dough hook attachment

In a small bowl, combine the water, yeast, and sugar. Stir and let stand until foamy, 4 to 5 minutes. Add the mixture to the bowl of a stand mixer. Add the salt, 2½ tablespoons melted butter, and ½ cup flour. Stir with a wooden spoon. Continue adding more flour, ½ cup at a time, until 2 cups are added. Return the bowl to the mixer fitted with a dough hook attachment. On medium speed, add the remaining flour, ½ cup at a time. If the dough is too sticky, add a little more flour.

Turn out the dough on a clean, floured surface. Knead the dough for 5 minutes, then take a small piece of dough and pull it in all directions. If the dough tears, knead longer; if it stretches, the dough is ready to shape.

Cut the dough into 8 pieces. Roll each piece into a length of 24 inches. Make a U shape with the dough and overlap the ends, then flip them back along the curved portion of the dough and press lightly.

In a large pot, bring the water and baking soda to a boil. Preheat the oven to 450°F. Line 2 large rimmed baking pans with parchment paper.

Boil the pretzels, one at a time, for 30 seconds, then remove them from the water with a slotted spoon or kitchen spider and place on the prepared pans. Brush with the beaten egg, melted butter, and coarse salt to taste. Bake 15 minutes until dark golden brown. Brush with butter once more. Serve with mustard.

TRES DEAN is a writer from Richmond, Virginia. He authored the 2019 essay collection, *For Your Consideration: Dwayne "The Rock" Johnson*, and several comic books such as *We Ride Titans*; *Eternal Warrior: Scorched Earth*; and *All Time Low Presents: Young Renegades*. His work is regularly featured in a list of publications that includes *GQ*, *Vulture*, *The Rake*, and Highsnobiety. He currently lives in Los Angeles with his cat Cash who, like him, is very easily distracted by cool cars when they drive down the block.

ACKNOWLEDGMENTS

To Ryan, Stewart, Andrea, Rob, Matt, Joanna, Sarah, Belia, Simone, Jess, Laurie, Noor, and E. Thank you all for turning a city into a home. *Salud, mi familia.*

INSIGHT
EDITIONS

PO Box 3088
San Rafael, CA 94912
www.insighteditions.com

Find us on Facebook: www.facebook.com/InsightEditions
Follow us on Instagram: @insighteditions

ISBN: 979-8-88663-271-2

Publisher: Raoul Goff
SVP, Group Publisher: Vanessa Lopez
VP, Creative: Chrissy Kwasnik
VP, Manufacturing: Alix Nicholaeff
Designer: Leah Bloise Lauer and Gavin Motnyk
Editor: Sami Alvarado
VP, Senior Executive Project Editor: Vicki Jaeger
Production Manager: Deena Hashem
Senior Production Manager, Subsidiary Rights: Lina s Palma-Temena

Photography by Waterbury Publications, Inc.

ROOTS of PEACE   REPLANTED PAPER

Insight Editions, in association with Roots of Peace, will plant two trees for each tree used in the manufacturing of this book. Roots of Peace is an internationally renowned humanitarian organization dedicated to eradicating land mines worldwide and converting war-torn lands into productive farms and wildlife habitats. Roots of Peace will plant two million fruit and nut trees in Afghanistan and provide farmers there with the skills and support necessary for sustainable land use.

Manufactured in China by Insight Editions

10 9 8 7 6 5 4 3 2 1